"Where you gonna go? W.........

Almost helpless, I lay there, broken, almost defeated. Trapped and tied up like an animal in Elfwood, a psychiatric facility where your parents dump you off like trash when they have given up.

My parents were newly divorced, I had only had a miserable breakdown because my father had thought it best that I go to the police, and give them details on the brutal rape that had happened to me one summer. Rape was supposedly one of the valid admission tickets to this place. I had multiple breakdowns over the matter.

It was supposed to be a safe town, the whole reason my parents moved us there in the first place. We had lived in a city, prior, with stabbings, motorcycle gangs, drugs… and then moved to a snobby rich little town which was one of my parents' worst decisions. I would have rather lived in the city with crimes, than the snobby little rich town. My new friends in my new town were psychotic, mean, nasty, and these were the kind of people that would invite you to sleep over, tie you up, and tell you that you were playing "victim" until it was time for your parents to pick you up. Now, I really literally was tied up, by a stranger, in a hospital, by a woman who abused her powers, and loved it.

My instincts told me this was "wrong," but I was almost certain there was nothing I could do. There were phone numbers on posters that hung on the walls to report hospital abuse, posters of abused people lying cold in a corner with tears soaking down their face. "Call if you have legal questions about your hospital stay." I held on for as long as I possibly could, so I could possibly one day make that phone call.

I had to pee, and it was an emergency. The woman twirling her gold necklace with her bony fingers heard my screams, but ignored them. I looked at my wrists that were badly bruised. There were hot tears stinging my face, showing my weakness to her. It killed me to cry because every tear that fell was her victory.

"If you don't let me up to pee, what am I supposed to do, pee on myself?"

"Yes, Mylee. I do not trust that you are safe enough to be untied to go to the bathroom."

There was sarcasm dripping in her tone.

It didn't make sense. Where was the other staff? Was I in a part of the hospital that was forgotten? Was this a nightmare? I couldn't pinch myself, because the ropes were holding down my hands tightly, and were burning my ankles. She liked to be called "Miss Betty." Ropes were illegal to use in a hospital setting, but this hospital had ropes.

That golden tooth that glistened when she smiled

disturbed me as she continued to read her book, and ignore my pleas. I had been tied down for having a seizure. The hospital had grown annoyed with my illness and the new motto was, "Just don't let her swallow her tongue."

Seven people held me down, as they injected me with tranquilizers. While I had seizures, I put up a fight when the staff grabbed me. The staff said my seizures were not real, after a few years, some of them were not real.

I had asked some of the other patients about my seizures. In the middle of a conversation, I turn blue, my eyes roll in the back of my head, my mouth shuts tight, I start turning grey, foam comes out of my mouth, I jolt, and then fight.

These seizures happened after I was raped. I always wondered if I had any thoughts while these episodes would happen. I wouldn't remember any of it. So, I would be sent to a "regular hospital," get CT scans, and be sent back to the ward. Sometimes, I had a seizure in the machine that scanned my brain.

Elfwood staff had grown tired of the "process." The new way of handling it was putting me into a "psychiatric hold." It was easier for them, so they could avoid the ambulance, and the whole transfer process. I went through roommates like a baby goes through diapers, and this week my roommate's name was Alice.

She felt bad for me, and told me that what these "caregivers" were doing wasn't legal, but I had no idea what to believe. I had thought it was just the way here. I didn't care about anyone I met in this place. I literally hated everyone.

My sister made up this big story that she had a "phobia of hospitals" that never existed, until I went into the hospital. What a coincidence! My parents were not allowed to visit me because the doctors and staff didn't want them to see my bruises, my bloody noses, my cuts from their nails, my purple eye sockets, or my significant weight loss.

They stopped feeding me while I was sent to the V-wing, so I wouldn't have to use the bathroom. I was bulimic anyway, so, no food to me, was not a real loss. The funny part is, I would prefer to be beaten, than to return home.

****

With all of the moving we did as a family growing up, I recall never feeling "home." Any time I got comfortable, it was time to leave again. I should have never unpacked my belongings. I guess my parents felt that a new environment would heal their inevitable fate to break up.

I can't recall "fun." All the bad stuff outweighed my select few happy memories. A trip as a family was always ruined by fighting. My dad would have to pull over and make my mother sit in the back seat with me, and my sister in the front seat. It wasn't just our fighting, it was their fighting, too, that required the predictable "pull over."

One of my family members would play games called, "Suicide," and tell me to walk through a pricker bush until I reached the fence, and if I had survived, I won. The pricker bush was right next to the fence, and scraped me all over my body, I was bleeding everywhere, but in order to win, I had to at least touch the fence.

My cousin would try to drown me in my grandfather's pool, and called holding me underwater "fun," and if I wanted air, I was a "baby." Another family member tied me up to a raft and flipped it over. I stopped breathing, and there was a woman who hated to swim that had a phobia of water, luckily there, dating my grandfather. She had to jump in, to give me mouth to mouth. While I gasped for my first breath of air, the one who flipped me over on the raft said we were "playing lifeguard." They still laugh about it, even though I never thought it was funny. I was at a very young age, with a very unnatural thought, "They should have let me drown."

****

Miss Betty untied me to let me use the bathroom. When I got up, she slammed the door in my face, almost smashing my fingers, and stuck her face in the tiny window in the door. With her golden tooth shining, and her laughter ringing in my ears, I peed on the floor.

My bladder stung from holding it in for so long. She opened the door, and said, "Now I have to get someone to clean that up! Why would you do that, I would have let you use the bathroom, Mylee!" I knew someone must have been behind her, for her tone to change to Miss "Innocent" Betty.

I kneeled down to the floor, licked up some of my urine, and spit as much as I could into her face. I laughed in such in evil way, that I couldn't recognize my own voice anymore. I thought for a second that I was finally changed into the monster they treated me like.

I was locked wildly into a hidden world, where no one would believe the nature of these people that were supposed to help us. So what else was I supposed to do?

She picked up the phone next to her desk and called a code orange. A code orange is when a patient has lost control, and they need assistance from any staff that wasn't busy to hold you down against your will, and inject you with a tranquilizer.

As staff entered my room, and saw that I was cool as a cucumber, the doctor came in last and asked Miss Betty why she had called a code orange.

"Mylee asked me if she could relieve herself in the bathroom, and urinated on the floor instead!" Like a childish lying tattletale. Of course, refusing to mention the part where she slammed the door in my face, and cackled like the Wicked Witch of the V-wing.

This was one of numerous times Miss Betty tortured me, and got away with it. Every time, I planned to get revenge, but she had the upper hand, being considered "authority." I was told I was one of the "lucky" patients, because other children were hurt, too, and couldn't (wouldn't) talk of her abuse.

Humiliation should be the last thing to worry about in here, but there are some horrors that are just left unsaid. When you were placed into a hold, your ending fate is to be stuck with Miss Betty, and she became more creative over the years, with her cruel and unusual torture.

This time, I was in the V-wing for only a few days.

I had turned 18, so was moved to the adult ward. It was a blessing, even though I did not believe in such things. This also meant I would possibly never see Miss Betty again, because she only worked in the children's ward.

The minute I returned to the "normal" adult community, there was a new patient named Henry. He locked sad looking eyes with me and gave me a pathetic "I want you" stare, and I didn't want to feed the pig, so I looked away. I also thought for a brief second that maybe he didn't want to have sex with me, which perhaps my ego may have conjured that one up.

I wasn't afraid to be with the adults. I felt they should fear me, because I had been institutionalized and my animal-like mentality conformed to this way of life. I fell asleep pissed off.

Hours later, I felt my underwear sliding down my legs. There was someone on top of me. I felt the tip of his penis touch my vagina. I looked in my darkened doorway, where I planned to run, and there was a tall male staff member masturbating. Before the patient, Henry, could fully penetrate me, I screamed, and kicked him with my knee in the balls. He threw up on my floor.

The hospital had police officers come to the ward to speak with me and the male officer seemed to be aroused by my story, so I told them I didn't want to press charges. I didn't want to continue telling a tale of hospital erotica to a careless perverted man who wore a badge.

I left the room where they had been recording my story on a tape recorder. Henry was moved to another ward. Suddenly, as I turned toward the hallway, I bumped into a girl with tattoos and a shaved head. We watched Henry leave the ward, with staff assistance, and he stared at me all the way out of the door.

"Welcome to the adult ward." She said.

"Does this stuff happen a lot?" I asked.

"Yes," she replied with a smile.

"I'm Mylee," I said.

"I am Ashley." She responded.

I instantly felt uncomfortable. I was a bad ass in the children's ward, but now I was everyone's piece of meat in the adult ward? So I was going to be molested and raped by patients and staff?

I looked around me, and everyone had deep scars and cuts all over their bodies, rope burns on one girl's neck, a girl dancing seductively in front of all the male patients, with their small boners apparent in their hospital pants. This was a freak show, a mad house. These patients actually belonged here.

The feeling of fear turned to a brief sickened arousal, and I was suddenly very excited about being here.

That's when I made the decision to scream at the top of my lungs. I wanted to test the code orange up in the adult ward.

Instead of being in a room alone where a staff can hurt you, there is one solitary room, and the three other rooms include a roommate. Honestly, you are tied up next to each other. I was lucky; I had a roommate tied next to me. I thought it would only make sense to attempt to strike up a conversation. She didn't respond. It was worth a shot.

The man in the doorway who was the "constant observation patient care associate's" name was James. He was a staff that seemed human. In my whole stay in these kinds of places, I never thought a staff member could seem friendly, likeable, down to earth, but he was.

He was reading a newspaper, looked up at me, and had this memorable grin on his face, joker-like, playful, and evil? His grin enticed me as he asked, "So what's your deal? I gotta watch yo ass for a couple days so what's up?"

Coming from the children's ward, with my bad ass image, I didn't want to God forbid seem nice, so of course, I let out the Mylee response.

"NONE of your DAMNED business."

I liked to use cuss words, but he deserved a mild version of me, for now.

"Oh come on, girl. Don't be that way!" he grinned again. "I'm James. I already know your name is Michelle." He said.

"Never call me that. I hope no one heard that shit. Call me Mylee or I'm not speaking to you. I'll let you know now I'm very good at the quiet game, and when I get nasty, I get nasty, so it's your choice who you want me to be to converse with me." I barked.

"Okay Mylee. Wanna rap?"

What an odd thing to say. How are you supposed to

respond to that?

"My name disappeared like vapor, can't look me up in the newspaper…"

James had to interrupt my corny rap attempt.

"I'm sure you were going somewhere good with that, but can you beatbox?"

"No." I admitted.

"Well we have a couple days together, so my mission is to teach you."

What is this guy's deal? I am stuck in a room with an almost dead roommate, she won't speak to me, and this guy's willing to teach me to beatbox, my other option is boredom. Seems interesting, I guess. Part of my problem is letting people in, so what's the worst that can happen here?

I learned to "beatbox" in three days. He told me of

his children, their favorite TV shows, their humorous behaviors and mannerisms, he even got me to admit that I knew how to draw, so he suggested writing comics, so I did. Spending time together almost made me forget my past, my problems, me…

The doctors saw I was improving my behaviors, so stuck me back with the adults, and I missed James. I was afraid again to return to this section. Then, the weirdest thing happened. A peculiar man came up to me.

"Ever do crystal meth?" I was sitting down reading when he walked up to me. He was scratching his arms. He looked strikingly familiar, but being out in the boondocks, there was no way he could have gone to my school. This man had a goatee, with shaggy hair, and dots all over his body, a drug addict.

"Meet me in the bathroom and I'll hook you up," he stated.

I had no idea why, but I met him in the bathroom, as the staff walked by, the moment after their fifteen minute checks. I didn't know if we were supposed to have sex, I didn't know if he had crystal meth. I don't know what came over me.

At that point in my life, I had tried every drug that had not been in a needle, so I sat down on the toilet, and waited. I knew he had seen me go into the bathroom, but the moment I began to ponder, he quickly opened the bathroom door, pulled out a tie he ripped off from his robe. They no longer use robe ties in hospitals to my knowledge.

He tied up my arm, tight. From behind his back, he pulled out a needle, and flicked it a couple times. His eyes were rolled up in the back of his head, his tongue on the side of his mouth, as if he were "concentrating." Before I could refuse, or comment, he jammed it into my arm, and plunged drugs into my vein without warning. I couldn't explain that I didn't like needles. I couldn't explain that I thought he meant he had pills. My eyes rolled back and that's the last thing I remember before I fell asleep on the toilet.

If I got high, I have no memory of it. I woke up in my bed, the same bed where I had been violated before I went to the V-wing. You'd think my room would be changed out of curtesy to forget the traumatic event with Henry. Not a chance.

The sun was beaming into my eyes. I scratched my ass, and walked out into the hallway. I saw the boy with the shaggy hair, who was hyper and full of energy. Life flooded his pink cheeks, obviously not the person I met last night.

"You gotta fill out your menu if you want breakfast," He said, and smiled. This person seemed very familiar.

"My name is Rich." He smiled again.

"You mean, when pigs fly?"

"Yeah!"

This was the man I slept with one of the times I was released from the hospital.

"What the heck did you give me last night?"

"Drugs. My friend brought them in for me."

"Duh, drugs, but what was it?"

"Did you like it?" he asked.

"No way, and you did it so fast, I didn't have a say in the matter, and you could have asked me if I was ready. Something, damn… None of the nurses in here can find my veins at all…"

"Well you looked like hell, and I heard what Henry did to

you. I was trying to help."

"Well I don't need that kind of help. Don't fucking do it again," I barked.

I snatched a menu out of his hand and walked to the back of the ward. Fuck him. Who the hell does he think I am, anyway? Stupid ass. I regretted sleeping with him, and I never found out what he gave me in that needle.

****

Moving to a new town was going to come with some adjusting. I was not excited, because in my old town, I was the center of attention, which I was proud of and even cocky about. The second I stepped foot in that school, the bullies swarmed me like flies.

The clothes I wore weren't cool, my backpack, my pencils, my hair; everything about me was made fun of on my very first day of school. These people's parents had money so they dressed completely different than the urban area I grew up. I wasn't used to people hating me, and I wasn't very good at handling things like this. This was only 4th grade, and I never believed this could happen to me, or my sister. She probably was teased more than me. I used to hear her crying in her room.

****

In Elfwood, my roommates changed liked diapers. Ashley was one of the more memorable people in my deluxe luxurious stay in the nut house. I wanted to ask her why she had a buzz cut, but it was none of my business. The change from the child wing to the adult wing was a dramatic difference for me. Sometimes I thought to myself, am I maturing? So, I'd do my thing and act out so no one else would think so.

Ashley was a very violent person, but a sweetheart to me. Now, she was memorable because if a boy had shown any love or sexual interest in her, she would beat their ass. To me it was funny, and odd. I knew I liked to repel relationships as well, but I never thought of beating the thought out of them.

When someone "code oranged" and put into the V-Wing, their bed and room in the community stays where it is. So every time she got in trouble, since she was my roommate, I'd have the room all to myself.

I used to practice singing all alone in my room. I still had my hacky sack, and practiced kicking it alone. It actually does get depressing when you're roommate is gone, and I imagined how others felt in the children's ward when I was stuck for days with Miss Betty.

I had a very overwhelming feeling that it was probably a vacation for them when I was gone. Having too much time to think was turning me into a person who actually gives a damn about myself, other people, this place, other's feelings. I didn't want to admit I could think a little clearer and I was possibly growing. There was no way I could figure out a life for myself once I got out of here. That thought alone scared me. I thought I wasn't afraid of anything for a long time.

Ashley came back from the V-Wing a few days later.

"Ashley, I've been here a very long time."

"Well you couldn't have been here that long, this hospital is an acute hospital," she stated.

An acute hospital is a place to temporarily treat you for mental illness and transition you back home, or to another facility.

"Did you know there is a children's ward here, and a geriatric floor, and an addiction floor, and..."

"Well I know about the addiction floor, I had a boyfriend in there once," she said.

"Did you know about the children's ward?" I asked.

"No, I haven't heard of it."

"Well I was transferred here from the children's ward, and I've seen things, horrifying things. They use ropes instead of the cuffs to tie you down. Just like out of a horror movie, the staff hurt you, spit on you…"

Ashley looked as if she didn't believe me, and said, "Well I know the restraining methods here are pretty fucked up, but they don't use ropes on this floor. That's illegal."

"If I told anyone, like my parents about it, and tried to do something about it, the staff would just hide the ropes, I think. The tables have the regular restraints attached, so it would be pretty easy to remove the ropes if they were being sued. I tried to call the police from the patient phone, and my 9-1-1 call went straight to the security desk, and I got restrained for it. They have 9-1-1 calls blocked in here."

"So, you're telling me there's a children's ward? That alone sounds illegal."

"Well it's not illegal. Parents are excited to dump their kids off thinking it's a nice place to be babysat and have behavior corrected. The kids change into monsters from the sickening ways of being treated down there. I turned 18, so they moved me up here."

Ashley continued to look skeptical and the subject faded away as it was getting late and it was almost time to fall asleep. I was in the children's ward for years. The psychological damage it has done has haunted me eternally. I wish I was making up a crazy story for Ashley.

That morning, while we were all eating breakfast, James, the beatboxing staff was in the regular community.

"James," Ashley called him over.

"Is there a children's wing in this hospital?" she asked.

"Yes, Ashley," everyone looked up from their meal in shock. Everyone began talking at once.

"I would never send my child to a mental hospital, especially a place like this!"

"What kind of parent would subject their child to an environment full of dangerous people?"

"If I was placed in a children's psychiatric ward, you best believe I would never talk to my parents again!"

    I didn't want to finish eating my food. I got up and ran to my room and slammed the door, which was pointless because our doors have no locks, no knobs, so it just swings back open.

    Ashley came into the room after me. "Mylee, why

did your parents leave you in a children's ward for so long? What did you do? Why are you here?"

That same old asshole Mylee that lived inside me got up off my bed and replied, "Mind your fucking business you hairless freak. You didn't want to believe that there was a children's ward, so back the fuck off. None of your fucking business. Don't talk to me for the rest of the time you're here, until your loving parents get you out of here."

There I was. I was wondering why moving to the adult ward made me soft. Maybe James helped with calming me down, but I knew for damned sure I was tired of being nice. It was time to be the way they taught me to be in here, a heartless monster.

****

"Dad, I have no friends." I cried on the downstairs couch. I had a group of friends, but after moving to the snobby rich down, I realized there were "cool kids." I wanted to be "cool." My dad insisted, "If you want friends, make friends. What else do you want me to say? Call them. Here's the phone book." I grabbed the phone book and dialed one of the girls that I thought was in the "cool group."

We didn't know each other, never spoke before, but she liked talking to me. Her voice sounded different on the phone. We talked every night. She told me all the things she hated about the girls in their "group."

They were very sexual and I was nine years old, too young to think that was "cool." I thought it was disgusting. I got what I wanted after a few weeks on the phone; she invited me to sit at their lunch table. My "friends" were devastated that I was "leaving them." I had a best friend, and I had grown ready for a new crowd.

Only, when I finally sat at their lunch table, all they

wanted to do was talk negatively about my old friends. They made fun of them so coldly, they laughed. They actually tossed their heads back, like a bad teen movie.

I told them after a week that I didn't want to sit with them anymore. It wasn't a "cool" feeling. I went back to sitting with my "old friends." Only, they couldn't figure out why I wanted to sit with the "cool kids," and never treated me the same way they did before. I couldn't help but think, "Who are these people? Where did my friends go?"

****

Rich found his way to my lunch table. I had been so behaved; I'd earned the privilege to eat downstairs in the cafeteria. He had a plate of French fries.

"That's all you're eating?"

"Yup." Every day, he asked for a plate of French fries. I grabbed a salad with fat free dressing. James, the staff, ate downstairs, too.

One day, James sat next to me, and said, "You've been here two months and all you eat is salad. Girl, eat some food." He bit into his greasy cheeseburger, with ketchup oozing onto his plate, and walked back to the staff table. I guess I couldn't realize my eating disorder was creeping up on me. So, I ordered hummus with my salad for the next week, and eventually stopped eating just salad, and tried to eat like everyone else.

"You left my house. You had my number. Why did you sleep with me and never try to contact me again?" He asked desperately.

"I don't know." I recalled a time when we first met how I had a girlfriend in the "children's ward."

Carrie. She had committed suicide and I slept with Rich most likely from feeling vulnerable from her simple departure from the hospital, I hadn't known she committed suicide yet. The sex was great, but I had a very deep fear of abandonment when I met them both. I had grown tired of being dumped, or starting a relationship, just to end up in the hospital again. I never attempted to make a permanent plan with someone.

Randomly, I woke up in the hospital one day with a girl I'd never seen in my life laying in my arms. Ashley had been in the V-Wing (as usual, she started to be in there more than me) I screamed, she screamed and she jumped out of my bed and ran away down the hall. These were the silly things I had just grown used to. Her excuse was, she could only sleep if someone held her gently. I admit, I did have a few good laughs those days in Elfwood. I'd grown used to crazy.

****

I had to earn the privilege to leave the hospital to go

to my own high school graduation. I missed prom. I was constantly trying to find successful suicide methods on the computer. My "friends" had abandoned me when I was sexually assaulted. My new friends weren't friends at all.

Feeling alone was something I couldn't grow used to. I grew up needing people like an addiction. I felt safe when I had so many people on my side, someone to talk to, to vent to, to laugh with, and to cry with. People in school would ask me, "Why are you so different?" They couldn't, wouldn't try to understand. I only saw monsters around me. The people that once loved me were sitting at the cafeteria in groups, separated into genres.

I needed money for drugs to erase the memory of middle school and elementary school, when things made more sense, so I kept the lunch money my parents gave me, and didn't eat, so I could smoke pot. No one noticed the days I skipped eating, because I had no one that cared to notice.

A very well-known boy in my school who was loved by everyone, committed suicide, and I was told to "shut up about my depression." To stop crying and whining, that "no one cares," and that his suicide meant more than my feelings. I was crying "too loud" at his funeral service.

One of the boys from school embarrassed me in front of everyone at the funeral service, and screamed loud enough for everyone to laugh at me, "No one cares about you. Don't try to make his suicide about you." That night was the first time I ever cut myself.

****

My roommate Ashley was very funny, silly, & nice, but I gave up caring about her when she pissed me off, making me feel like I was lying about the children's ward.

Eventually, I talked to her again. There's really no choice in here. Everybody's crazy amused her. She reminded me of Carrie, in the way that even though we were stuck in Hell, that there was still humor. The staff couldn't take that away from us. I wasn't attracted to her, though, which was a big surprise for me. I seemed to get attached to everyone I met. I fell in love with almost everyone, and just needed people.

I received a letter one day from my cousin, a male cousin, and we never really talked in person. I think maybe his mother forced him to write to me, who knows.

Shockingly, he related to how I felt. He sympathized with my problems, and I was told my whole life to stay away from him, that he was trouble. At family gatherings, I was very afraid of him, actually. He wrote sensitively, and it brought tears to my eyes.

In the midst of my emotional moment, some fat,

ugly, troll of a women snatched my letter out of my hand. "No one here likes you." She stated her words like a well-known fact.

"Give me back my letter." I looked up into her eyes.

"Make me," she groaned like a beast.

This could have been my moment to show this place the heat of my anger. I am short, she was huge, but I knew I could take this bitch.

Instead, that night, I went behind the nurses' station while the nurses were tending to a screaming patient down the hallway, leaving the nurses' station unattended. I grabbed my file. I had a hint of curiosity to read my file, but I crept into the troll's room. She snored like an old man, I lifted her mattress while she slept, and stuck my file underneath.

The nurses were going wild that morning. Instead of

announcing that while they were not supervising the nurses' station, someone stole from behind the desk due to their lack of responsibility, they called a huge community meeting. They were in the wrong and they knew it, and they had announced that there were to be room searches, immediately. No one was allowed back into their rooms. Rich walked over to me, "What did you do," he asked.

I smiled.

The community room's volume was thick with shouting and nervous tension. Everyone put on guilty faces. I had a nervous thought for a second, I walked over to Rich.

"Please tell me you got rid of that needle," I pleaded.

"Of course, I'm straight. Just tell me, what did you do?" I smiled again.

The staff came out of the beast's room with my folder in her hand, and called her name. I wanted to laugh, but had to keep my cool and hold it in. Next, they called my name. We walked into the visiting room together with a male staff, my favorite, James, the beatboxer.

"Mylee, I want to let you know, Sandra took your file last night and hid it under her mattress. I am bringing you into the room, because your privacy had been violated. Sandra, your level has been dropped which means your visit with your family will not be happening this afternoon. Dropping to restricted status means that you will not be able to have visitors for two weeks until you improve your behavior. We also found this." He sounded so professional.

He handed me my letter.

"Because of how seriously violating her privacy is… we are moving you to another building so pack your things. Mylee, you may return to the community."

As I walked out, he winked at me, and she glared at me.

I never saw that bitch again.

****

The boys in school were making a group in the hallway, laughing about something. I had been holding textbooks, wearing my sunglasses. I had stopped eating after I was raped, and wore sunglasses in school to "hide." I didn't see his foot, and I tripped, spilling my books everywhere. They kicked my books each time I bent down and reached out to grab them.

The teasing had reached a point where enough was enough. I told my parents what was going on, and they reached out to the school principal. Most of the teasing had stemmed from the internet, and the teasing had turned to bullying.

The principal said, "Sorry, it will never happen again and we can't do anything about online bullying."

The next day the boys were obviously spoken to by the principal, because this time they were shouting, "He should have raped and killed you, you fucking slut."

This time police were called into the school. The end result was, "she should just change schools." No one got in any legal trouble, my parents were fed up with the school's lack of discipline, and as I was cleaning out my locker, an old friend came up to me and asked me what was going on. We had been friends in middle school, but after the rape, all of my old friends took a "no one talk to her or believe her" oath.

I missed her kind eyes, her laugh, and how fun it was to have friends. I told her I was leaving the school and told her why. She ran up to the boy who tripped me, grabbed the hat which he'd loved and worn since middle school, and gave it to me. I was very confused, but said thank you. It almost gave me hope that maybe there were still a few humans somewhere that cared.

His hat was light baby blue with a sports team on it, and written in marker under the rim said, "I love you baby," from one of the girls that turned on me.

I set it on fire when I got home.

****

We all sat in a circle, passing a coin, saying our goodbye, good luck, farewell, to Rich. He was leaving the hospital, and the coin was passed to me. I passed the coin without saying a word. He left, and that was it. I wondered if I should call him if I ever returned home.

It was a quick departure, and I didn't want to make a big deal of it, but as the security guard opened the door, and I watched it lock behind him, I felt something in my body. My nerves were shot. I swallowed the lump in my throat. I ate French fries that afternoon.

A new boy arrived. When you leave the hospital, someone instantly replaces you. He looked afraid. He was very ugly, and the guys began throwing old milk containers at him, calling him the usual "clever" names, homo, etc. For the first time, a rare occurrence, I made it a mission to try to be his friend. A male staff walked over to me, and said,

"Mylee, would you give him the grand tour? She has been here a long time she knows the ropes."

It was a funny thing to say. It bothered me and made me feel paranoid when he mentioned ropes. I had a flashback of Miss Betty.

I got up, and the timid boy that looked very afraid as I held out my hand to give him a handshake.

The staff member said, "There is no touching here, Mylee, you know that, this is Kyle."

He replied, "Good because I hate germs."

It was so strange how quickly we became best buddies. He told me how much he hated his mother, how he had a phobia of water and germs. The men and women of the ward were so cruel to him. The teasing was so bad, that he would probably get diagnosed with PTSD from the teasing alone. People get diagnosed with PTSD from coming to and experiencing Elfwood.

I got lost in a mini paradise with my new friend. Weeks flew by, with nothing but laughter and I had been so well behaved that I was allowed to have beads in my room to make jewelry. Kyle had been on his best behavior as well, and earned the privilege to come into my room and make jewelry with me, as long as a staff could watch us, so we couldn't have sex.

The thought of sex never crossed my mind with him. He was like the loving sibling I never had. My dad came to visit me, and he came and sat down in our visit, and my father could tell that there was something obviously wrong with him, but my father couldn't see his heart. He saw him as annoying, even called him disturbed.

I guess I just couldn't see the disturbed nature that everyone else saw, but me. I liked to sing in the hospital, so we put together a talent show. Kyle cried in front of me, explaining that he had no talent. I held his hand and told him to show the jewelry off as his talent. He smiled and I saw his face show pure joy. That night, I was singing on a karaoke machine in front of everyone for the talent show. He stood up, grabbed the wireless microphone, and sang with me. Who cares if he couldn't sing, it was awful, I mean awful, but he was happy.

One of the male patients threw water at him while he was singing. His phobia of water made it seem as if he had been shot by a bullet. It was cruel. He looked at me. I was filled with rage. I saw the boys from my high school tripping me in the halls. I saw myself drowning and being laughed at by my own family. I saw Miss Betty slamming the door in my face.

The male patient was very large. I believe he used steroids prior to coming to the hospital. He was a big, muscle head, beefy, tall giant. He stood up to fight Kyle. I punched him in the stomach. I kept punching him. I threw a fist into his face, I kept punching and scratching, he even turned around, and I kept beating his ass. They called a code orange as I punched the back of his head. I took off my shoe. It was a sandal. He had shorts on, the kind you wear to the gym, so they were thin shorts. I shoved the sandal in his butt crack and kept pushing, and pushing it up his asshole through his pants. He was screaming, and he threw up his hands.

I yelled, "I thought Kyle liked it in the ass, guess you were the pot and Kyle was the kettle!"

The staff picked me off of him like a scab; I didn't put up a fight at all. I was laughing hysterically as he picked the sandal out of his ass like a wedgie. As they pulled out the needle, I saw Kyle in his doorway. He mouthed, "I love you," to me as I fell asleep.

The few days in the V-Wing were worth it, but when I got out and returned to the community, Kyle was sitting alone at the table in the kitchen area. He was staring at the water dispenser. His eyes were very beady and he was holding a bracelet that I made for him. As he was rocking back and forth, he started screaming.

"Water's dirty. Dirty. DIRTY!" He lost control the minute he locked eyes with me. The staff called a code orange. I watched as they pushed him to the ground. He was screaming, "The ground is DIRTY! The GROUND IS DIRTY!" The staff pushed his head into the ground so the floor would muffle his mouth. They stepped on his head.

They put both of his wrists behind his back, held up the needle, pulled his pants down, and the guy that had the sandal up his ass looked at me and said, "He still likes it up his ass."

I grabbed a fruit, a pear. I said, "You fucking fruit."

As he turned to run away, I threw that pear so hard to the back of his head. It exploded. Did I mention I played softball? There was pear juice all over the floor. The nurse rushed over to me, "Mylee! Did you just throw a pear at Matthew's head?"

"No," I said. All the staff was so busy with Kyle, that she was the only staff who had seen it. "I'm going to get you a pill to calm you down. You know you shouldn't be throwing fruit. Come on, Mylee."

"Weren't you working on the children's ward?" I asked. She looked very familiar.

"Yes, when you first came to Elfwood, I snuck you outside and gave you a cigarette, Mylee."

"Really? Why? I don't remember that."

"Because I knew you needed one. By the way, nice shot to Matthew's head! He needed somebody to beat his ass, but I didn't think a girl would do it!" Her nametag said "Marie."

I watched the rest of the staff carry poor Kyle to the V-Wing. I never saw him again, but I read in the paper later in life that he died in a school shooting. He was the shooter.

****

My grades were above average in middle school. I had so many friends, I was in Girl Scouts, and I went to church. I'd even given violin class a chance, folk art lessons, cross country, softball; I was a very busy girl. I was running late for the bus for school as I was painting my nails.

The bus stop was literally right outside of my house. I heard the bus driver beep, so I grabbed my sister's nail polish remover and all of my nail supplies, jammed my homework, my project and my Girl Scout uniform into my backpack.

As I was minding my business on the bus, the annoying new kid who had called me "the ugly red head girl" had been staring at me, like he usually did. I decided to give him something to stare at. I took my nail polish remover and cupped my hand around the top and inhaled, pretending to be getting high. There was a lot of people staring and a girl screamed, "Michelle is getting high!!" (I had earned the nickname "Mylee," later on in life.)

That day, I was called into the principal's office for my very first time. "I searched your locker and I found drugs." She slammed the nail polish remover on the desk. "How long have you been a huffer?"

I didn't respond. I had nothing to say. "You are suspended, and I'm calling your parents. I'm giving them a video that you need to watch about the effects of inhalants. Drugs are strictly forbidden in this school."

I burst out crying, "I do my best at school! I wanted to get a scholarship! I've been working so hard!" I cried.

"This is going on your permanent record; make sure you watch the video because I will have the health teacher quiz you on it when you return."

As I walked into the classroom to get my books, everyone was staring at me. I screamed, "The good girl is being suspended! Whoever ratted on me will BURN IN HELL. Pass the message." I was hurt and ashamed.

I went straight to my computer when I got home. I did some research, and something phenomenal happened. I found information that a person could only get high from "acetone" content in nail polish remover. I had printed the articles that had been had found, and prayed that night that the nail polish remover had no acetone content.

My parents said that I didn't have to watch the video. They were disappointed in me when I told them that I had pretended to smell it, and pretended to get high as a joke, but were convinced there was no acetone in the nail polish remover my sister had bought. I fell asleep with hope; we were going to the school the next day for a fair fight. I crossed my fingers that the principal still had the nail polish remover in her office.

I presented my case with my mother. We gave her the articles, and showed her the links to my discovery. The principal looked flushed and began talking very quickly. "I am not going to be taken for a fool. How do I know you didn't run to the store and buy a bottle of 'non-acetone' nail polish remover?"

I responded, "You took it out of my locker yesterday and slammed it on your desk yesterday morning. You still have my sister's nail polish remover and she wants it back."

"Oh, right," Now she really looked flustered. She reached into her office cubby, where her ugly coffee cup and her ugly grey jacket were, and there was the nail polish remover. I crossed my fingers.

"Non- acetone," she said. "I don't know where to begin…"

My mother who had been silent said, "So a person can be suspended for pretending to get high? This sounds like a defamation of character lawsuit to me. My daughter should not have been suspended, perhaps detention, but not something that will remain on her permanent school record. This is a pretty serious 'silly mistake,' do you have children? Is that what it is? My daughter gets outstanding grades, never got a B before, she gets sick over studying too hard, and this is the treatment from the school she is going to get? Maybe I should look into taking her to another school. It's bad enough the Girl Scout leader works with me, and treats my daughter like shit because she doesn't like me. Let's go Michelle."

"If I may," the principal said. "Let's look at her suspension as a one day absence. Clearly, I have made a mistake. I have the power to take this off her record. It scared other students on the bus when they saw her wafting the nail polish remover; everyone looks up to your daughter. I was trying to set an example for the other children!"

"So can I go back to class?" I asked.

"The day is halfway over. Just take another day off. All of this must have been punishment enough. I know from talking to your teachers at our meeting about this that you suffer from extreme anxiety," said the principal. My mother yelled, "Let's get out of here. I see why you have such anxiety. The people around you are trying to intentionally bring you down. This whole thing was ridiculous. You're better than them. You'll show them when you're valedictorian." We drove home.

I walked into the house with a stomach ache. I walked downstairs and placed my sister's nail polish back onto her dresser. I never painted my nails again, unless someone offered to do it for me. I didn't know for sure if acetone vs. non-acetone meant it was drug free. I didn't care, my research worked and I got out of trouble.

This was the start of my downfall. I've always wondered how my life would have been if it weren't for that day. I spiraled into a whole other person. I truly believe "Michelle" died on that bus. It had altered my perception of who my friends truly were. I made it a mission to never talk to anyone in school again. I began a new hobby. I began writing.

****

Lying in bed, listening to an old woman fighting off a code orange made a very vivid flashback that had been barricaded in the far depth of my memory. Before I could blink it away, I heard their voices in my head, "Michelle just relax, and you'll like it." I closed my eyes and my teeth made a grinding sound as I clenched my mouth shut. I felt alone.

They were doing whatever they wanted with my body. I drank so much that night I just kept saying to myself, "This is your fault. This is the price of drinking." My arms and legs were being held down. I closed my eyes and he finished; there were both boys and girls taking their turns. I felt the steaming burning on my ankles and arms. I was being held above a fire and the first thing that popped into my head was an old cartoon, where a human was being roasted over a campfire.

As I lay in my bed in Elfwood, I rubbed the scars on

my arms, along with cigarette burns, from when I was being used as an ashtray that old night in the tent.

Ashley was still my roommate, and she saw me rubbing my scars and asked me what happened. The horror of it was so terrible that I had to write the whole night down on paper for my lawyer and the police who were recording me. At least I could look down at the paper, so I didn't have to look in anyone's eyes. That was how the sunglasses came into play. I didn't want anyone to look at me.

"Which scars are you talking about?" Instead of my usual, "mind your fucking business."

"The ones near your wrist and the ones on your ankles."

She couldn't see the ones on my upper arms because of my shirt. I thought for a while if I should say anything to her. I was silent, but she still sat there in anticipation. Kyle left, and I felt that every time I became close to someone they would leave, or die. With my usual response, I answered, "None of your fucking business."

"Fair enough. Wanna do something?" She asked.

"Like what?"

"Let's break out of here." She stated.

"I've tried that so many times." I responded.

"I have an idea. Wanna act all nuts and get the booty juice?"

"Why the fuck would you want booty juice?" Booty juice was the needle the doctors/nurses pull out during a code orange. The thought had NEVER crossed my mind that a person could actually enjoy it, or get high from it. "If you tell me why you shaved your head, I will tell you where one of my scars came from." I said.

"Oh that's easy. If you came to groups, you would have known that already. I eat my hair."

I thought for a minute that she was kidding, and then I remembered where we were.

"One of my scars is from drinking blood. I was into the vampire scene. We cut ourselves and drank each other's' blood, I'm not going to tell you where that scar is." I wished I was kidding. "So you like booty juice?"

"No. I like sleeping. If I'm asleep I don't have to obsess over body hair, I rip it out, lick it, then I eat it. No sleeping meds work on me. The only thing that works is booty juice."

"Well I hate to break it to you, but it comes in a pill form. So, you could just tell your doctor it relaxes you, and he will just give it to you. That's the medicine I am on."

"No way! You're kidding me!" She was dumbfounded.

"Maybe I should just run this place. They make all the patients so much crazier than they have to be," I joked.

A guy poked his head in our doorway.

"I'll give you money if you girls make out right now," he said pathetically.

Ashley got up, slowly walked over to him, grabbed his head like she was going to passionately kiss him, and then planted her knee right in his throat. As he screamed down the hallway, we heard. "Staff assist. Code Orange. Return to your rooms. Staff Assist."

She got what she wanted; she got booty juice.

****

"Michelle, what the hell are you doing? You look like you've been snorting cocaine, what is going on? I'm telling if you don't give me any answers."

I had finally moved my computer into my room, and I stayed up for four nights, writing continuously. "I've been writing," I replied. "I haven't gotten any sleep lately."

"Well I have been talking to one of my friends about an illness she has been diagnosed with, and I think you need to see a doctor. It's called bipolar disorder. I'm talking to our parents in the morning." I didn't really care that my sister was worried about me, and figured this was just some bullshit she spit out. When I got out of school the next afternoon, there were my parents and sister on the couch, with a VHS movie on the table.

"Just because her friend has a disease doesn't mean it has anything to do with me. Leave me alone!" I screamed and ran upstairs and slammed the door to my room. I didn't eat dinner that night, but I waited for everyone to fall asleep, and I crept downstairs, grabbed the tape and ran back quickly to my room, as quiet as humanly possible.

I didn't want to believe I could have something "wrong with me," but the tape clearly described my personality. I never let them know that I had watched it, because I tiptoed back down the stairs and placed the tape back onto the table. I couldn't sleep for another night, and I hated to even dream the idea that my sister could possibly be right, but she was.

****

I was extremely bored. I had no one to torture, so I made a very weird decision. I decided to attend group. I had done it before in the child wing to make a few escapes out of here. This time, it was pure boredom. I would get nervous about going to groups, because that was the step to go home.

So, my very first group in the adult wing was called, "Meditation." I walked in and there were people on pillows, one guy laying down on the floor on a mat, a girl playing with meditation balls. I walked out. The group counselor ran after me, "Why, Mylee! You didn't give it a chance!"

"Go rub some meditation balls up your clit." The lady looked very timid, shy, and nervous, and my comment probably ruined her month.

I was playing hacky sack in my room when I was called into the doctor's office. I hadn't met him yet. He looked strange, overdressed, and I found it odd that a nurse hadn't accompanied him in our meeting. "Sit down. Relax," he held out his hand. I sat down without shaking it.

"So, you told the counselor running meditation group to go rub meditation balls on her clit. Am I correct?"

"Yes. Are we done?"

"I was wondering where you could possibly come up with a comment like that. Do you do that to yourself?"

"EXCUSE ME?"

"Let me rephrase the question. What method do you use to masturbate?" He licked his lips.

I ran from his office. I remembered that poster hanging in the children's ward that had a phone number to report hospital abuse. I approached the nurses' station, "I need the phone number to report hospital abuse." The nurse with long black hair looked over her glasses at me. "To report what?" she asked.

"None of your fucking business!" I yelled.

She talked into the microphone, "Staff assist. Code Orange. Return to your rooms. Staff Assist."

I woke up in the V-Wing tied to a table. James was in the hallway watching me from the door. The nurse with the black long hair and glasses told James that we needed a moment. She shut the door behind her, and my 'roommate' tied to the other bed was asleep.

"You were in the room with my husband. What were you going to report him for?"

She had a glass of water in her hand, a notebook in a pocket on her red blazer, and a pen in the other pocket, on the other side. "He was asking me what I masturbate with."

"Lies, lies, LIES!!" She screamed. Reminding me of Miss Betty, and sure enough, she poured water all over me. She grabbed my hair, "My husband would not be interested in you. Report what you wish, but I'd be careful if I were you."

She opened the door, and James came into the room and untied me. "Did she just pour all this water over you? You're shivering! What happened?"

My "sleeping" roommate answered, "Her husband hit on Mylee. She didn't like it, threw water on her, and then threatened her."

James gave me a new blanket and new patient gowns to change into, and let the nurses' station know that he untied me. He also slipped the phone number to report hospital abuse to me. "Use it when they not lookin," he whispered.

"According to the staff and doctors' notes, you are schizophrenic." The lady on the patient helpline said. "That means I cannot take your report because you do not know the difference between truth and lies and it's hard to determine what your reality is. Under these circumstances, I cannot take your report."

"WAIT!" I gasped. "That's not fair! You have to take the report! You have to take every report!"
"Sorry to shed reality on the situation, Mrs. Mylee Weir, but I am not going to waste an investigation on false information. Have a nice day!"

Nothing was ever going right for me. I felt defeated. I was stuck, and I finally wanted to go home. We were a broken family, it was never going to be the same, but I didn't feel safe in the hospital anymore. I used to call it my safe place. It was turning into a living nightmare. I knew once I was home I would just want to go back to the hospital, but I decided I'd take my chances.

I had a social worker and when I met with her, I discussed my doctor's perversion, how the staff masturbated and watched as a patient sexually assaulted me, how the nurse poured water on me, how Miss Betty tortured me for years, and how I didn't feel safe in Elfwood in the adult unit. She had a team meeting with the nurses without the doctor, and told me the next morning that I could go home.

My mother picked me up. I wasn't adjusting well to the new environment. It wasn't our big house in the snobby rich town. I couldn't sleep, began cutting myself again, drawing bizarre pictures of flashbacks, with bleeding stick figures and demons.

I begged her, "Please don't send me back to Elfwood."

She called my psychiatrist and he prescribed a very large dose of sleeping pills. I still could not sleep. I heard a man in my thoughts, "We washed the sheets. All of the evidence is gone. So your little plan to open your big fat mouth is shot to shit now!" His laughing echoed burned into my memory. I felt like I was on fire again, so I ran a cold bath. I got in, lowered my head under the water, and saw my cousin drowning me. I jolted up and ran around the apartment, completely naked.

I lay down after a while, ran into my room and pulled the sheets over my head and closed my eyes, remembering how the rapists thought at first that I was passed out and asleep, again I jolted up. I needed to go back to Elfwood.

My mom brought me to the hospital. I was admitted back into Elfwood. I grabbed a pen off the visitor sign in clipboard and went into my room. The bed next to me was empty, because they try to admit new people in the morning. I bit off the tip and the back of the pen and blew the black ink all over my wall. I drew a demon, the demon I kept seeing since the rape.

The next morning, I slept late. I was back in hell. The last time I blew ink all over a wall, I was trying to impress my girlfriend. I wanted attention, and I got it, from her and from the staff. This time I awoke to a painter in my room.

I guess the staff didn't call me into a meeting, or address it, because they knew I was sick. It was my first day back, maybe they understood my pain.

During my long stretch of hospitalizations, I lost track of time. I didn't care about a future. There were no future plans for me. Some say I wanted to die for attention, but the reality was that my future plans were to successfully commit suicide.

I had cut myself so I wouldn't hurt anyone else. My anorexic phase wasn't a cry for help; it was a suicide attempt, just much slower and more painful. I didn't like who I became. I always wished I could be born again, to get a new life, like a reboot. My dreams included any job that would surround me with people who admired, adored, or just simply loved me.

I didn't feel love the way I used to after I was raped. I became a big part of "who's telling the truth." There was no support for me. I had come out of the hospital and told both of my parents about the molestation that went on when I was just a child. No one wanted to believe that either, so I gave in and told them it was all just a story. No matter what I said to anyone, there was always doubt. Therefore, I felt like I had nobody to vent to, and no one who believed me. My aunt was the very first person to make the quick decision that her boyfriend would NEVER touch a little girl.

I had so much hatred for everyone around me that I never felt safe anywhere I went. I didn't feel like the hospital was healing me, or even helping a little. When someone tried to be helpful and understanding, and made me feel like I can trust them just a little bit to open up, they'd ask questions, making me feel like I'm being interviewed by the police all over again. My paranoia was getting stronger and my sickness was only getting worse.

After the painter was done painting the wall, my new roommate entered the room. Ashley was history, and of course, I didn't get to say goodbye. Her name was Jill.

"I just came out of prison. Are we fucking tonight or what?"

I laughed my ass off. I always prided myself on acting tough, making that first mean impression. I laughed, got out of bed, and decided breakfast sounded like a very good idea. I didn't answer Jill.

As everyone was chewing louder than the TV, (another inconvenience which I'd grown used to), Jill grabbed the phone, and made a very loud phone call to "Paula."

"Bitch, I just got out! I still got the anklet; they said I belonged in a nuthouse, not jail! NO!! Of course I don't have a roommate! NO!! Yeah right, sure. Well at least you don't have to send me money anymore. Yeah, you're welcome, GOODBYE! Yeah, love you too."

Lucky me, I got the lesbian that was fresh out of

prison. Of course, sex ran through my head all day. She had dark curly hair, glasses. She was funny, abusive to the other patients, which to me was incredibly hot. Jill reminded me of myself, in too many ways. I wondered if the two of us having sex would kill us both.

I took a hot shower, thinking maybe Jill wasn't physically my type. She was no Carrie, for sure. When I walked into my room dressed and ready for bed, she knocked me over onto the bed and pulled my pants down. "Jill STOP!" I said. She was going to wreck me if we didn't slow down.

"What's the problem? I thought you wanted to fuck. You didn't answer so I assumed…"

I wanted to go to sleep, honestly, I was too tired. There was finally someone who was more sexual than me.

"Jill, you can't just pull my pants down. I like to kiss first."

"Oh, come on with that bullshit. I have a girlfriend!" She said.

"What the hell is that supposed to mean?" I was appalled.

"Come on. Fuck the fancy shit, I need to get laid I don't want no sentimental ties," Jill stated. I was instantly turned off. I told her to stay away from me and fell asleep.

I woke up the next morning to Jill's naked vagina on my face. Smiling like a distorted clown, looking down at me, she was grinding her vagina so hard, I thought I felt her bone. My nose started gushing blood. I grabbed her, and threw her. Her head smacked the floor. It made a very concerning noise. She was knocked out.

I never knocked anyone out before. I left her on the floor and sat on my bed, holding my knees nervously. It was very early, because I heard the nurses going room to room, drawing blood. They do that around 6 am. I thought maybe that she was dead? The cracking sound on the floor wasn't something you hear every day. What seemed like hours were probably just a few minutes, but Jill woke up. I ran out of the room, into the dining area. It was far from breakfast time, and there were more people awake than I thought there would be.

Marie, the nurse who congratulated me for throwing the pear at Matthew, walked over to me. "What's wrong, Mylee?" she asked. "I want a room change." I responded. "Jill snores so loud, I will never get to sleep."

I know I was taken advantage of, for what seemed like the millionth time, but I didn't say anything. Being raped as a teen, the whole court process took so long, and the people involved received ten years of probation as their punishment, while I received a lifetime of problems, a lifetime of pain, hurt, mental and emotional torture.

I was hurt and violated back then, and since then,

when it happened again, after that cop smirked while I reported that second time in my room, looking enticed, I never reported assault again.

Later in life, I did report more assaults, but never followed through with going all the way to have them arrested. I became silent. Some dumb asshole said, "If you were raped MORE than ONCE, then I'm sorry, I don't believe it. If I was raped, I would NEVER let it happen again to me."

Rape is not about choices. If I "let it happen," it wouldn't be rape. By not reporting the occurrences, I knew it was wrong, and could happen again to other people, I knew I wasn't doing my duty as a woman and a human, but I became withdrawn when it came to being violated. I had developed the mentality that, "I must have done something to deserve it."

My family sure wasn't helping in that department. I

was blamed by my family for the rape in that tent that night. It's crazy how when something traumatic happens to you, you find out rather quickly that people would rather deny that it happened, from fear.

Everyone wants to believe the world is such a safe place. Friends and family sort themselves out. There are believers, and non-believers, enemies and allies, people and monsters. I gave up on loving people with my whole heart.

"Mylee, why is there blood all over your face?" Marie asked. I had forgotten that Jill most likely had broken my nose.

"I have no idea why there is blood on my face," I whispered. Our rooms were changed. My new room had no roommate, just an empty bed, for now.

****

We were in language arts class. There was a girl

that was considered "popular, and "cool." We had a writing assignment, and we had to read our papers in front of the class. When she stood up, she shared about feeling like an outcast, feeling alone, bullied even. The class started laughing.

That evil boy that used to stare at me on the bus during the nail polish remover incident, the new kid, well his name was Jack, and he was laughing extra hard. I couldn't bring myself to laugh, even though I knew why everyone was laughing. She was loved by everyone, the most beautiful girl in school, in my opinion, but she couldn't see it, and I know how it feels to want to hide from everyone, to disappear.

Jack was an awful person. Living so close to each other forced us to hang out after school. My character started changing when I met him. He was cruel. He believed the tragedy of the twin towers was funny. He even drew a picture of the twin towers on cereal boxes and set them on fire.

When the boy in my school had killed himself, Jack said, "He was just another dumb jock anyway. He's lucky he killed himself, because I would have done it for him." When I got suspended for the nail polish remover incident, it all started because he was staring at me, ready to insult me, like he always did. He had very violent fantasies, and was very descriptive with details of how he would kill people, if he could get away with it.

When I talk about friends betraying me, in the worst of ways, this shell of a person, Jack, hurt me the most. The "party" where I was raped, consisted of a group of people, that DID NOT include him. He was not invited.

While I was going through the court process, he actually had the audacity to make a false police statement, saying he was there, and that it didn't happen.

Later in life, when I discovered social media, I reached out to him, and asked him why he hated me so much, why he went an extra mile to lie to the police. His response was crude and shameful, including the words, "I'm not sorry, enjoy your web of chaos."

****

I watched as one of the patients stood by the window, swaying back and forth, almost like she was dancing. Every day, she stood by the window, her mouth open, dry with chapped lips. She never sat down, and smelled the way I would imagine death would smell.

She wore the same outfit every day. I tried to talk to her once, but she kept swaying back and forth, without acknowledging me there. I tried to ask James why she didn't come to the cafeteria with us, why she stayed upstairs. He couldn't tell me, due to patient confidentiality.

I stayed up one night, and I walked to the dining area, where she stood, still awake, still swaying, back and forth. I colored on pages until morning. A team of doctors walked in with a stretcher. "Caroline, ready to go to ECT?" one of the doctors asked. She didn't respond as they lowered her onto the stretcher. As other patients arrived to the dining area, I walked over to the nurses' station, and asked if they could print me a definition of "ECT." If you behave, you can request printouts of information online, as long as it was appropriate. She handed me the paper:

"E.C.T. stands for Electroconvulsive Therapy. It is a procedure, done under general anesthesia, in which small electric currents are passed through the brain, intentionally triggering a brief seizure. ECT seems to cause changes in brain chemistry that can quickly reverse symptoms of certain mental illnesses. It often works when other treatments are unsuccessful."

In my very first hospitalization, I had actually asked if something like this existed. I was told yes it existed, but it was banned from the state, so not to worry, that it wasn't an option in the hospital. I had seen this in a movie, and it traumatized me, and gave me nightmares.

Watching the effects of this on Caroline made me wonder if this was legal. The doctors came in the morning, when no one was awake yet, she wasn't improving, she was almost a complete zombie, so why were they doing this to her? Her depression could literally be sniffed out from the next room.

I knew that ropes were banned from hospitals, and I was told this medical procedure was banned; it made me wonder if this was hospital's staff was addicted to torture. After all, even the helpline for hospital was ineffective. The patients were at least released, so that was a good sign. I decided to try to behave that day.

I talked to some of the patients at lunch that afternoon about this shock treatment, and they said that this hospital was one of the only hospitals around that still do it. It became a fear of mine rather quickly. "It's only done if you tried all kinds of meds and nothing works. It's used when they just give up hope for you," some ugly dude said.

A girl floated into the room with dark hair, and piercing blue eyes underneath bangs. Her body was scarred, and instantly rage flooded into my veins. My teeth gritted, and a lump formed in my throat.

"What are you doing here?" I shouted.

The girl began to cry and ran into the bathroom. Carrie was my ex-girlfriend that wrote me a suicide note. I never doubted her note, because she knew how much suicide notes bother me, and the doctor in the children's ward had told me he was saddened when he heard of her loss, confirming her loss. The girl came out of the bathroom with all of the makeup she came in with running down her face.

Marie, the nurse, walked over to her, then walked her over to me. "Mylee, this is Katie, she is going to be your roommate."

"Oh cute, new nickname?" I asked.

"What are you talking about?" she replied.

"Don't play games with me, Carrie."

"Who's Carrie?" she asked.

Marie responded, "Mylee, her name is Katherine, her nickname is Katie."

"Okay, sure, I'll show her around." I didn't know what was going on, but I decided to play along. I showed her the hospital unit, and gave her the rules, then finally showed her the room. When we come with belongings, they are searched and put into paper bags.

Anything that is not allowed or valuable gets held at the nurses station's safe until it's time to leave. The rest thrown into brown bags. So, she dropped her brown bags onto the bed and plopped down. "I'm so tired," she said.

"You came from the emergency room?" I asked.

"Yes. I tried to kill myself with pills, they kept me awake, pumped my stomach."

"Well don't think you're special, we've all been through it, you're not unique." I barked.

"Why were you calling me Carrie? What was that about? Am I missing something?" she asked.

"Stop the bullshit, Carrie. What, are you in the witness protection program now? You changed your name, and you can fake it to everyone else, but I'm not buying it." I was beyond pissed off. She sat silent for a while, and eventually turned her back and fell asleep.

****

"But mom, I really wanna go to this party! All my friends are going to be there!" I somehow persuaded my mother to let me go to my friend's birthday party. I didn't like to eat cake, I just desperately wanted to see my friends away from school.

It was 4th grade and my parents were very strict about me sleeping over people's houses. I would hear about how much fun my friends had at the movie theatre, at festivals, etc. My parents didn't trust me away from them, because they thought something horrible would happen.

I packed a lot of things for this sleepover because I had never been to one before. I made sure to bring my childhood stuffed animals, Cindy and Mr. Happy, one being a yellow pig, the other a smiley face with arms and legs. As a child, all the way until I started blooming into a teen, I had an obsession with smiley faces. My room was covered in anything to do with smiley faces.

So, as I'm dragging my luggage into my friend's house, everyone was gathered around a bowl of chips, talking, laughing. A few more people arrived as the radio was blasting music. I was unaware my friends were in dance classes together, so it made me jealous as they were practicing dance routines. I had always wished my parents would allow me to do some kind of activity. Eventually, I was in almost every activity.

This night, I wished it would never end. The girl's parents were extremely kind, and funny, and it made me wish I could stay there forever. Then, the night came.

I held my stuffed animals tighter and tighter, and the girls that were spread out on the floor in their sleeping bags climbed on top of each other and started kissing. I knew some of my relatives were gay, but I felt very upset that these girls were horny so young. It went from kissing to the removal of clothing. I turned my body in the other direction to try to close my eyes and pretend I was somewhere else.

The blonde girl sleeping next to me had her big wide blue eyes wide open. She had a water bottle with a big block of ice inside of it. As the kissing got louder and more obnoxious, she said, "This water bottle is you," and started licking the ice through the mouth opening.

I didn't care if the girls would hate me after, but I ran so fast up the stairs, where the parents slept. This was the bravest tattle tale I'd ever been. The girl's mother came running down the stairs, and we all had to separate into different rooms in the giant house.

I didn't tell my parents right away about what happened, until something similar happened at the next sleepover I went to. Knowing my parents were right about sleeping over strangers' houses being dangerous, I refused to admit they were right. At the second sleepover, I called my parents crying and begging for them to pick me up. As I stood by the doorway, I held my stuffed animals, as my tears fell onto the floor, as I was wishing that we never moved to another city.

****

It was extremely hard to pinpoint the once specific reason why I needed to be hospitalized for so long. I became very good at blaming specific events, or people. I never wanted to take any responsibility for my inpatient stays. It was everyone else's fault. I knew there was something wrong for as long as I could remember. My reactions to all of these traumatic events weren't helping the matter. I know it wasn't my fault that I was raped, molested, beaten, tied down, teased.

I knew while sitting in my bed next to random switching strangers that I needed help. I knew I wasn't growing or learning from anything by sitting around, bossing people around, and starting trouble. I just couldn't point the finger at myself, or accept any help.

I didn't like my living situation; I hated everyone, so I could care less about going home. I had future plans at one point in my life. I wanted to be a teacher. I studied so hard I got physically ill. Once I got my first B, I stopped caring about school, because I was counting on a scholarship, knowing my parents could afford to pay for the kind of schooling I wanted. I began to feel like all I cared about was myself. It was the one word that could push my buttons, "selfish."

I grew up loving to share with my sister and my friends. My favorite holiday was Christmas because I loved buying presents for my family and friends. I received allowances, and spent my money on everybody else. So, the word "selfish" hurt me, because I never thought I could be called such a word fairly. Caring so much about never going home was the factor in my extremely long stays in psychiatric facilities.

It was Katherine that broke me. Once I truly believed she was Carrie, my mental state slowly deteriorated. I lost interest in being the clown or troublemaker in the ward, lost interest in food again, and became a cutter again. I stopped showering. I slept, all the time. Katie would make things in art group and bring them into the room as a present for me, and I just laid there, without making any effort to rejoin the community.

I believed finally that she looked like Carrie, but she wasn't Carrie. My dreams stopped. There weren't nightmares either. I slept just to pass time. There was nothing to look forward to anymore. I finally gave up, and felt defeated. My new doctor walked into my room. I was relieved that it wasn't the perverted doctor.

"Mylee, I would recommend giving E.C.T. a trial. You just aren't giving any effort to get better. This could change your life," he said. He seemed very nice, and looked like a mad scientist.

This was it. My friends gave up on me, and so had my parents, my family, and finally, the doctors. I explained to the doctor that I wanted to think about it because it was a major medical decision that could either ruin my life, or change it for the better.

As he walked out of my room, I sat up in bed, and cried. I cried for hours. I felt pathetic. Suddenly, something empowering happened. I remembered taking a physical fitness test in middle school, and one of the requirements required doing pull ups and push-ups. I couldn't do either of them, but I also remembered that I felt like I didn't really try. Everybody could give up on me, that's fine, but I wasn't ready to give up on me.

I kneeled onto the floor, and I did one push-up, pushed myself, and did a total of thirty, on my very first try. I pulled out a sketchpad and began to draw. I had to pull myself out of this depression. I asked the staff if I still had the status to go downstairs to the cafeteria. Being told I still had privileges, I joined the lunch line.

As I ate lunch, I saw the boys outside playing basketball, just shooting around, and I asked them if I could play, too. I threw the ball over my head backwards, while closing my eyes and made the shot from a very far distance.

The next day I played volleyball with everyone outside, and the day after, I played soccer. I used the hallways as my new walking track and walked circles around the ward, and I was also continuing my push-up routine.

My exercise woke me up out of a very bad depression, but again, I still didn't want to go home, but the doctor walked into my room and told me that it was time to go home.

I called my mother, and she drove me home. I was fairly certain that there was a chance that this could have been my last hospitalization, but I blasted the radio and I didn't want to say it out loud, I just wanted to enjoy the moment.

My mother and I got a very tiny apartment together. I didn't feel like it was the dream life that I grew up hoping for. I became familiar with the internet and made a decision that I wanted to be a musician, so learned how to make music on my computer from my karaoke tapes.

I didn't know how to write lyrics, so I just sang other people's songs, until I met a man through a mutual friend that played guitar. He thought my voice had potential, so we worked together to make music. He was married and I grew fond of his wife and we spent a lot of time together.

I felt like this was my new family, until one day me and him were alone in my apartment, due to my mother had gone somewhere. He pursued me in a sexual way, and I was so enticed by the moment, that I forgot about condoms.

We had pretty boring sex, and I regretted it so fast, that I was ashamed of myself, and never wanted to see him again. I knew I could never look at his wife again. The music was very important in our lives, so I continued to go to his apartment anyway, and met one of his friends. He was a rapper and had no place to stay, so my mother told him he could stay in her car.

I began to drink as a coping method from my guilt for sleeping with the guitarist, so I slept around. I lost track of time and self-worth, and when I didn't realize that my period never came, I had no way to track or figure out who the father was. I did not believe in abortion, but I held my breath when I took the pregnancy test, of course, it was positive.

The man who slept in my mom's car was a rapper, which helped entertain me, we spent a lot of time together, he made me laugh and I didn't want to tell him about the positive pregnancy test. We had slept together too. I was so embarrassed when I had to look my father in the face and tell him I was pregnant, but had no idea who the father was. My stomach grew as my worries grew.

The neighbors next to our tiny apartment were disgusting people, stressing me out, pissing me and my mother off, and the anger was not good for my pregnancy, so we moved away, again. This was a much bigger apartment, and we baby-proofed everything. My nesting period was over the top unhealthy; I lost a lot of sleep trying to make things perfect. I became paranoid, and I stopped taking my medication, because I was nervous it was going to hurt the baby.

My uncle had passed away, someone I lived with when I had no place to go, and I was so mentally ill, that I asked my father if my uncle could come over to help me clean and paint, even though he was dead. I started talking funny, which was a sign of being off my meds.

So, my parents made the decision to stick me back in Elfwood. I had an asthma attack and called an ambulance, and my parents told the doctor that I needed a psychiatric evaluation because I was pregnant without medication.

I was traumatized, and made the vow that I was never speaking to them again. Elfwood was a dangerous place for a pregnant woman, and no one seemed to care. The doctors and staff still treated me like an animal, without any sympathy for my pregnancy. A patient came up to me and grabbed me by the shoulders.

"You gotta get outta here, girl, if you don't get discharged by the time you're baby is due, they will take your baby away, that's what happened to me!" I wasn't due for months, so surely I didn't take her warning seriously, I knew I'd get out before then.

 The doctors kept changing my medicine. Every time a medication change happens, the doctors keep you in the hospital longer, to watch for side effects. The weeks passed, the months passed. I was ready to go home, I'd been behaved, well mannered, I had turned into an adult, but the hospital just wouldn't let me go. My mother told me to sign out and give a three day paper.

 A three day paper is when a court hearing happens for a judge to decide if you are stable enough to leave, instead of the hospital doctor.

I never signed a three day paper, my baby came faster than I thought she would. The hospital called DCF and my baby was taken away.

I was mad at everyone. My family betrayed me. I was alone, without the little person I kept safe from all harm for nine months. She was my new reason for living a new life, she was taken away without being given a chance to be a mom. She was taken right from the hospital.

When we had an assignment in school that required a writing prompt explaining what we wanted to be when we grew up and why, I wanted to be a mom. That's it, and was my dream, and now that opportunity was gone.

So, I stopped taking my medicine. I slipped into a psychosis. My father got me a lawyer, but the end result was: my daughter was given to my father. I finally felt like I belonged in the hospital, maybe forever.

When a person cries, until stomach pains occur, it doesn't touch the feeling of losing a child, or of staying locked in a psychiatric hospital with no way out. We all have our breakdowns, but to lose total control and end up in places like Elfwood, it's a living nightmare. Sure you can lie your way out, pretend everything is okay, fake it until you make it out, but how do you get better?

I wish a lot of things never happened, I wish I could have done things differently. Every experience instead of making me stronger, sucked life and time away from me, weakening me. I never had been to jail or prison at that point of my life. I've been told a psychiatric hospital is a hotel experience vs. a jail stay/prison stay. I would suck and grit my teeth when people would say I was living the life. I was losing my life.

Every time something bad would happen, I told myself something good might come of it, just to learn that something worse will be next. So, I lost faith. I lost my religion. Everything I believed in was gone. I didn't care about a future anymore. The hospital killed me. I felt dead.

I tried sometimes to learn, but I didn't feel any different after participating in treatment. My anger grew hard and cold and stuck with me. As tough as I made myself seem, every insult, every nasty word, stuck deep into my soul. Feeling changed into an animal was one thing, but my sensitivity never left me. So everything hurt me, I just didn't want anyone to know.

I got to the point in my depression, after losing my daughter, that I should commit a serious crime stay locked up for life, and hope someone would kill me since I didn't have the guts to kill myself successfully. It was the people I surrounded myself with that convinced me that I didn't want to go down that road. The doctor sent me home after I lost my daughter, not because I got better, but because there was nothing left for me at the hospital.

Maybe my parents thought I'd come out a changed person. I came out with resentment, and hatred. My rage was highlighted brighter than it ever had been. I was looking for a person to attack, either by words, or whatever worked for me.

I saw a set if kitchen knives, and right back to square one, I began cutting my arms, and made my way down to my legs. I knew being upset wasn't going to get my daughter back, but I couldn't snap out of it.

My father went and got my daughter's first haircut without me, I missed her first crawl, and her first words. My family including my cousins, aunts, and uncles, spoke to me like a fragile creature. I'd been locked up for so long, I was being treated as if there was something wrong with me.

I gained weight from medication, cut myself again, so started wearing long sleeves again. My parents accused me of throwing up all my meals. There were rumors spreading about me of how I was incapable of raising a child. I was so sick, and disgusted that these were people who I grew up believing would love me unconditionally. I couldn't decide what hurt me more, being slowly kicked off the family tree, losing my little baby girl, or being locked away with almost no visitors for so long.

I knew if anyone saw the cuts all over my body that I would be sent back. Finally, going back to the hospital became a phobia of mine.

I went to a few self-help groups, support groups, therapy groups, trying to find an answer, a lesson on how to smile again. The idea popped into my head that maybe I could cover my cuts with tattoos. I went to my tattoo shop and he said in order to cover my scars, I'd have to wait at least a year for the scar tissue to heal.

I had to stop cutting for a year. I cut myself to keep out of legal trouble, to not harm anyone else except myself. I needed a new release, and I needed to think fast. Of course I chose men as a sexual release, and it didn't work for long. I tried gambling, and my life turned into a whirlwind of even more problems.

I suddenly was obsessed with compulsive gambling; I dove in, and couldn't make my way out. The devil grabbed me and wouldn't let go! I stopped caring about people, I stopped worrying about DCF, didn't care about sex anymore, and my hospital was no longer my addiction. I fell into relationships by accident, and ignored them completely, no matter how wonderful of a person they may have been. As long as they had money, that's all I cared about. Years of gambling made me unaware of all my surroundings.

My boyfriend would buy heroin and scratch tickets for me. I even tried heroin, and told him that gambling felt better. I called some of my old friends sometimes when I stood on train tracks, waiting for the train to take my life. I was a loser. If I won, I gambled it all right back.

I never looked up from my scratch offs. I was buried in the high feeling I got from the rush of gambling. I swallowed pills numerous times. I jumped off of a chair with a noose around my neck, just for the chair to kick back and give me the chance to change my mind. I knew I was sick, and yes, big surprise, I was in and out of Elfwood, again.

They brought me into a section where we had to do chores. I fell in love with washing dishes; I loved the hot water on my skin. I thought to myself "I'm doing something with my life, I'm occupied, and I'm not thinking as much while I'm scrubbing these dishes."

Then it happened. Fred "Twich's" name was brought up in the kitchen. Twich was my high school sweetheart who had overdosed on heroin. I went from happy scrubbing pots and pans, to dropping a pan on the floor. I ran to my room, and threw up.

It seems that no matter happy and how hard you try to put some thoughts on the backburner, they somehow manage to accidentally creep up on you. He tried to solve my problems of cutting while he was alive, and tried to convince me to express myself through poetry.

I looked down at my arms, which I hadn't cut in a while. I was excited about moving on and getting tattoos. I felt a rush of happiness and wondered if Twich's angel was somewhere patting me on the back. The rush of the ocean waves where he proposed was very vivid in my memory. Rubbing each other's' face on his bed, the giant hug he gave me after I performed at my talent show at the school we shared, so many happy memories.

I know I haven't said it yet, but I was in the hospital for a gambling addiction. It was the same setting, the same scene, except we got to leave the hospital to go to meetings; we had chores, and the staff actually cared in this section of the hospital. I felt great in here; it was like a heavenly dream, being treated like a human.

I remembered Miss Betty spitting on me in the child ward. I could never blink those memories away. The memories of my whole life burned into my brain, forever.

****

I was a virgin in middle school, and the "cool kids" teased me, calling me "prude." I started growing boobs, and I earned a few nicknames, whatever clever names associated with boobs, because they were just so original. So, I taped them down. I was proud of myself, being in the chess club, having softball as an outlet. I would pretend the ball was their heads and crack homeruns down the field. I ran around the bases with a smirk on my face.

The boys were bad with teasing, but so were the jealous girls. My best friend told me over the phone how she kissed this one, and sucked that one. It was pretty pathetic, and it turned my stomach. Sex or anything to do with it grossed me out. I wanted to play, to pretend, to laugh, to be kid and everyone else just wanted to get pregnant; that's how I looked at it anyway. The girl I used to be before I went to hospitals, before things started falling apart, before I became someone else, loved the idea of love.

My mother told me what a gynecologist was, and sex scared me, kissing sounded gross, and I figured if I never had sex with anybody, I wouldn't need to be tested for anything. I didn't see the point in sticking something up my vagina.

I thought one of the boys in school was cute, looked him up in the phone book, and called him out of the blue. I didn't think he even knew who I was. We talked for hours.

My mission was to have a real boyfriend, one who would hold my hand, spend time with me, meet my parents, protect me, and dance with me. He had blonde hair and blue eyes. I remember feeling like the room was sparkling, and that I found my prince, and I would be able to get away from my family, and let love save me. He asked me to go to the movies.

It took a lot of convincing for my parents to let me go with him, and the answer was no, until his mother agreed to come with us. His mom showed up in the driveway, and I sat in the backseat with him. She made small talk with me, and I instantly got her approval.

We got out of the car when we pulled up to the theatre, and she said, "Okay kids have fun."

"I can't be in the theatre with him alone," I said.

"Your parents aren't here. They're not gonna know," she winked at me.

I felt it, this was it. I was going to kiss a boy. It was going to be awesome like a dream. I could finally be in the club of girls who have kissed a boy. He chose a seat in the back of the theatre. I walked up the stairs making a countdown in my head. 10….. 9….. 8….. I was going to kiss a boy.

I put a piece of gum in my mouth. I had seen in a movie two people kissing and the gum ended up in the other person's mouth. I was going to put my gum in his mouth.

      It happened.

      It was disgusting.

      Either he was a terrible kisser, or…

      Kissing was gross?

He tasted like hot dogs.

His mouth sucked my whole face.

I was horrified.

He asked me, "Do you know how to give a blow job?"

"No!" I shouted.

"I will walk you through it, I will teach you."

"No thanks." I responded. I wiped his spit off my face. My whole face smelled like spit. I wanted to call my parents and go home, but I had to sit with this disgusting kisser. He tried to kiss me again a few times, and I grabbed his hand and said, "Let's just watch the movie."

The next day at school, people in the hallways were making growling noises at me. Girls were calling me "WHORE!" Everyone was looking at me, people were pointing at me from their lockers, whispering. It really felt like a cliché teen movie, and I was the nerd being picked on. I went from being liked and admired, to the school dirt bag over night.

His best friend walked over to me. "It's pretty bad Michelle."

"What's going on?"

"He told the whole school you're so bad at kissing and blow jobs, that you used teeth, and his dick was bleeding at the movies."

"I didn't give him a blow job," I said.

"I hate to say it, but whether you did or didn't, he's a guy. If all the guys believe him, you're shit out of luck."

"But Tom, I'm a virgin. Make this go away? Can you help me?" I begged.

"He's my best friend, I know he's lying, but no one else

does."

"Tom, what am I gonna do?"

"You just should have never went out with him."

I stared down the hallway, and there he was, wearing his baby blue hat, grinning like a piece of shit.

    The teasing went on, and I became the school joke. My best friend lied and said she was in love with him, and that I purposely went out with him, because she liked him. Everyone made up or found reasons to hate me. I felt very alone. I figured out that everyone in my entire grade was done with me. Something that was nobody else's business affected my relationship with everyone in my grade. The only thing I chad to say in my defense was that he was the worst kisser, but I didn't want to stoop to his level, so I kept that part to myself. Tom did what he could, and tried to spread alternate rumors about him, but it failed. Nothing worked.

The transformation of my character was happening. People believing something that I wasn't took its toll on me. I guess that's why I started dressing differently. I dressed in khakis and tee shirts and taped my boobs for a long time. I'd seen it in a movie, and my boobs would bounce when I played soccer, so I strapped and taped them down, but it didn't really make too much of a difference.

All hell broke loose. I went to the mall and bought stripper boots and fish nets, and did not tape my boobs down that morning. I went to school the next day with my high heeled boots, fish nets, red plaid skirt, gothic make-up, and leather jacket. I didn't tell anyone the leather jacket was my grandma's.

The boys stopped teasing me for a while. The girls just stared. The girls started coming up with more sexual rumors about me, and all it did was make the boys more defensive of me.

My little plan was working. We went on a school trip, and it was a place that had a pool. I made the decision to wear a bright orange bikini. As the girls were making faces at me, I took my shirt off, walked over to the diving board, and dove in the deep end. I swam over to the ladder and there he was. Mr. Blue Eyes.

Mr. Terrible kisser was reaching a hand out to help me up the ladder.

I said "No, thanks," and shook the water out of my hair, fixed my bikini straps, turned around and pushed him into the pool. His baby blue hat was soaking wet floating away.

Everybody was laughing, and I didn't even care that I had a wedgie.

I decided to try to find Tom to tell him what happened. I threw a tee shirt on over my bikini, and searched all over the park. When I found him, he was playing lacrosse and told me he lost the lacrosse ball in the woods.

"I'll help you find it," I said.

I had a backpack full of snacks, underwear, and socks. We walked into the woods together.

"Do you know which direction the lacrosse ball went?" I asked.

"That way!" He pointed left.

There was a small clearing in the woods. He was walking behind me, and I stopped. I threw my backpack on the ground, and grabbed him. I had my hand behind his head and kissed him passionately. He put his hands on my hips, and we kissed for a while as he pulled me closer.

"You're a great kisser," he said.

At first, I didn't want to tell him that I kissed him just so he would tell everyone that I wasn't bad at it, or so it would piss Mr. Terrible Kisser off. When the kiss happened, all these feelings came up, making me feel like this should have been my first kiss. He didn't kiss me like a pig. He didn't tell the whole school. We had a moment and it was special. Tom ended up changing schools. He kept in touch with me long after high school.

I didn't care about the rumors in school anymore. I didn't feel like I had to dress any kind of way except the way that made me feel comfortable. I went to school simply for the butterflies in my stomach when I walked by Tom. For that one look, and one smile in the hallway, to remember that one moment, that would last a lifetime.

Besides, I got to set Mr. Terrible Kisser's hat on fire eventually anyway.

****

I walked up to the nurses' station and asked for my diagnosis.

"Do you need to see the doctor?" she asked.

"No. I just want to see my chart."

"Well, I can't just show you your chart without the doctor. We have to schedule a meeting with him to show him your diagnosis."

I had a few different diagnoses thrown at me. I've heard almost every psychiatric term associated with my name; they gave me almost every one. I was so confused, and every time I approached the doctor, it would be different every time I asked.

"You know what? No thanks. It's not going to change anything if I know or not. Forget it." I walked back into my room and threw a chair against the wall. No staff had heard me, so I threw the same chair against the other wall. I took a deep breath, and took the needle like a champion. Ashley was right about booty juice. Now I didn't have to think anymore.

****

"So what's your deal. What's with the scars?" I told him a little bit of why and he called me "nuts."

I had met someone that gave me the opportunity to live with him instead of my parents, or whatever family I had left. I didn't find him physically attractive at all, but it was an idea to at least become independent. I had just graduated from high school.

He liked to steal. He was trouble. It turned me on instantly. He spoke down to me like I was a moron. Living with him was difficult because he loved to blast rap music, and he had the audacity to tell his friends they could all take turns with me, with his permission.

Everyone laughed and looked at me like vultures. Luckily I never had been raped or even touched by any of them. It took me a long time to adjust to his very unattractive face. I made him have sex with me in the dark, so I didn't have to see. I learned every time he was gone, leaving me alone for hours, he was doing drugs.

One day he grabbed me by my throat and lifted me off the floor.

"Just because you live with me, doesn't mean you can just let yourself go. Either wear make-up and dress like a real woman, or I don't want to be seen with you in public."

That's when I should have left. Drugs became part of my life again, but I didn't leave. He told me he had to go to his mental health program to get bus tokens to sell for drugs. So he "allowed me" to come with him.

I was outside waiting for him when I reached into

my purse and pulled out our last cigarette, with the intention of putting it out halfway through, to save some for him. I was heavily plastered in make-up, dressed my best, just for the pig of a man he was. He came out of the program, and asked me for the cigarette. I gave him the half that was left. He grabbed both of my wrists, and pinned me to the brick wall, and grabbed my chin, slamming my head against the wall. He slapped me in the face, as my make-up poured down my cheeks.

Little did either of us know, but there was a female cop behind us. She grabbed him, pulled his hands behind his back. He screamed, "You better get me out of this!" The police officer lowered him into the backseat of a police car, and walked over to me.

"Please don't continue a relationship with that man. He's not a man if he can put his hands on you like that. Don't you think you deserve a better life?"

Dear Mom and Dad,

One last breath is the hardest one to take one last glimpse of the world. One last shot or opportunity to make. Everything around starts to twirl. The hardest thing is I was me, you were you maybe a dream, I was lost inside an empty mind. You can go on with the show, without you, who else would know? My fate has come and brought me to this time.

I am nothing, searching for something, relying on one thing that was never there. Goodbye.

-Mylee

Dear Mom and Dad,

Lying on this cold cement, stuck here on the floor, wound drips off my wounded head, my body is so sore. The flesh the lord has given me, it wasn't quite enough. My body rests in painful peace, it wasn't very tough. Misery and loneliness was supposed to be a shield. It was supposed to make the bullet yield. After being lonely in a world filled with bore, suicide was the only thing that protected me from more. After being laughed at, when people call my name, the only thing to laugh at now, is the writing on my grave.

-Mylee

I know I said I hated suicide notes, but I had written quite a few, started a collection, since Carrie died, and stashed them so no one could see. I filled a binder full of them and titled it, "Inside the Mind of a Psycho." When I started getting really into music, I had someone help put melodies to my poetry.

My music ended up giving me a motive to survive. My suicide notes were turned into art. I started to feel like maybe it was the time to begin healing, but no matter how happy I would start to feel, I just wanted to get lost in the gambling frenzy.

I thought if I won a fortune, maybe I could buy a beautiful place to live to get my daughter back, pay for the parenting classes I needed, buy a car, and become a human, all for my baby girl.

Instead, my soul was being taken, and I was penniless, left with no possible way to get her back. I felt like I gave up, like a big waste of life. The hospital was my only way of life. I had become institutionalized. I didn't know how to live a normal life.

****

After I lost custody of my daughter, I gave birth to another baby girl with a different abusive man, and I tried to kill myself with pills due to post-partum depression. This was it, believe it or not, just like that, this hospital stay was my last one. For real. I had ingested my charcoal shake, and I landed in Elfwood, but I wasn't there for long. I didn't get to say goodbye to James, or Nurse Marie, and as I walked out the door, I had no idea at that moment that I would never see the place again.

I dated another guy for a while, and he offered to help me get my life back together, by living in his house with him, and my children were welcome there, he was going to FIX MY LIFE! I was so excited, but as I was getting out of his van one day, I hit my head.

There's just this section of my life that is a blank spot. I had suffered temporary amnesia. The doctor felt it was best I recover at home, so my mother took care of me, as I did not know who I was, that I was a mother, who she was… or that I had been to Elfwood.

I don't know how long I was "gone."

One day I remembered everything all at once, walking up a hill with my baby's father. I asked him where my new boyfriend was. He said that I had lost my memory for a period of time, and my new boyfriend said it was "too much for him to deal with."

I couldn't understand what I was doing walking with him, and I burst out crying, because I tried to remember anything, and it actually have me a painful headache trying to remember, but those memories never came back.

I made a very hard decision to give custody to his parents, I finally accepted the fact that I was perhaps at that time, not in the right frame of mind to take care of two lives, when I couldn't take care of my own.

Soon, the memory of Elfwood became a haunting chapter in my life. My nightmares would jolt me awake. I couldn't believe how I was capable of surviving the physical, mental, and emotional torture that went on in that building. I couldn't appreciate any of it. Soon, over a long period of time, I tried to look at the whole mess as lessons.

My strong beliefs and opinions were based on real life events that I made it through. I ran into the staff at fast food places, the mall, and saw some of the patients eventually. I researched my diagnoses, and I wanted to get better. I tried to find humor of the whole thing, but it was too sad to find it genuinely funny. I did blame my family for a very long time.

I dreamt of the beat of my heart while running through the woods with Rich, the taste of Carrie's lips, the beautiful beach where Fred proposed. I knew for certain that the bad and good memories would bother me for a long time, so I voluntarily made the decision to attend therapy.

****

It took years for me to admit to someone I had been molested as a child, but I never had the courage to tell a soul that the reason I was throwing up in the backseat of the family car, was because I was seeing things. As we drove on the highway, the trees moving by so fast made a person appear in the woods. He always ran toward the car, with a knife.

I knew he wasn't there at a very young age, but I kept seeing him, and I knew that something was wrong. I always asked myself,

"What is wrong with me?"

"Why am I the only person who can see him?"

"Why is this happening to me?"

When the car came to a stop, the man figure would disappear. Inside the house, he never appeared. It was only in the car that I saw this man. He had worn a straw hat and overalls with a white collared shirt.

The whole time I was in Elfwood, I refused to talk about it, or mention it, because I didn't want to be judged, or laughed at.

The question would come up, "Do you see things or hear things?"

So, I would lie, "Of course not."

I wanted to be helped, but I didn't want to ever say out loud that I was seeing things. I was ashamed of myself. I thought I would be admitted forever. My phobia of cars was the reason I had agoraphobia. I wanted to stay indoors at all times, because that's where I was free from the monster farm man with a knife. I drew him everywhere. The pictures scared my mother.

Eventually, I admitted to my outside therapist after I left Elfwood that I see things. My whole life, I had the phobia of being sent back to the hospital for saying a word about it, and wasn't the reaction I expected. It was a revelation. He got down to business and sat in his chair differently, asking all of the important questions a professional should ask, and he told me to have a nice weekend.

I wasn't going to be admitted? He was actually going to help me? The psychiatrist asked me questions about it, too, and immediately gave me the correct medication that I needed probably my whole life, and I felt better, and all it took was honesty and bravery.

****

"Mylee, you know you can't smack the other kids in here in the face with books. Look how red Charlie's face is now!" I was in the children's ward, where I had gotten away with so much, for so long, and I told the nurse to shove a book up her ass and threw it at her.

This was the first time I had ever been placed in a psychiatric hold. I hit the floor faster than I could blink, and the nurses pulled down my pants and shoved a needle in my ass cheek. When I opened my eyes, I tried to get up, but I was tied down, by my wrists and ankles.

"My name is Miss Betty, you're in my world now. I don't take kindly to disrespect and if you do, you will pay the price."

An elder African lady bent over me, lowered her head to me and spit in my face. It dripped into my eyes, burning. I couldn't wipe it off, and closing my eyes made it worse. She sat down, laughing, and opened a book.

"I'm going to tell the next person who walks back here that you spit on me," I said.

She stood up. "You'll do what?"

"You're not gonna get away with spitting on me."

"Oh you think so, huh? Who do you think they'll believe? I worked here for thirty years. You're just a typical nutcase to them!" She walked over, put her hand on my stomach, and spit directly on my face, again. A lady walked by with a clipboard.

"How's it going in there Miss Betty?"

"We got ourselves a difficult one, she keeps trying to spit on me, but she's getting it in her face instead."

The nurse walked over to me, pulling out a needle.

I started screaming, "NO, NO!!!"

"If you don't like needles you will learn to CALM DOWN AND BEHAVE." The nurse injected my arm with medication and I fell asleep, with Miss Betty's spit all over my face.

I woke up and the room was blurry, and there in the corner was Miss Betty, reading. She saw me waking up.

"You're going to learn fast that I am the boss, and you'll learn to respect me."

She got up out of the chair and walked over to me. "Just remember, you're the pathetic one," she said, "Psycho."

When I was released back into the community, I asked around about Miss Betty, and no one wanted to talk. No one wanted to be specific about the humiliation she had the other patients endure.

This was my first lesson that from this point forward, no one was going to believe a word I said about any staff abuse that went on with the patients. It also enlightened me that now that I was admitted into a psychiatric hospital, nothing I said anymore would be taken seriously by anyone.

****

My flashbacks were getting out of hand, I was out of the hospital, and flashbacks were just getting worse. I remembered the first time being let back into the children community after being with Miss Betty in the V-Wing. I couldn't keep up with conversations, I couldn't think, my thoughts were racing and I couldn't keep up with my own thoughts. My hands were shaking, and I kept asking people "Am I making sense?"

A girl walked over to me, and asked me how I was feeling. I thought she was a cop. As I was eating lunch in

Elfwood in the children's unit, I lost my reality. Living in a haze, where letters and numbers jumped off paper in my school books, the room was always spinning, and my teacher kept asking me if I was okay.

The hospital had a school. There was a radio playing meditation music to help kids relax while they did their schoolwork.

I was swatting myself.

I felt like there were bugs all over me.

I started screaming.

All the kids around me got up and exited the classroom.

I couldn't calm down.

This was the only time I wanted to go home.

A nurse came in with a needle.

I didn't want to see Miss Betty again, but I just couldn't calm down.

My new therapist looked at me, asking if I was okay. I blinked away the old memory.

"When will my life get back to what it used to be?"

I asked.

"Life may not become what it used to be, but it's up to you, to make a better new life."

"I keep having flashbacks of the hospital, the rape, the bullying, I can't control them."

"Well, I'll speak to the doctor to tweak your medicine a little, but you've got to relax. You can't keep thinking about the past, because it happened already. That's why it's called the past," he was making sense, but I knew his advice only helped for a little while, then I'd go right back to my old thinking, and have trouble sleeping until I saw him again in a week.

"Do you think hypnosis will work to erase everything out of my mind?"

"No. Honestly, I don't think it works like that. We can talk out your problems, get them out, on paper, however we have to do it, but you need to let them go, somehow."

I didn't want to utilize his help, because anytime I told somebody what I was thinking, I'd be recommended to have a psychiatric evaluation. All my thoughts landed me on that lonely bed in Elfwood. I believed my thoughts were better off bottled up.

"Mylee, why don't you try making friends, join activities, go to church, find a hobby, anything to get you to stop thinking about all the bad stuff?"

"I don't want friends."

"Why don't you want friends?"

"Everyone hurts me," I said.

"Believe it or not, the whole world isn't bad."

The time was up and it was time to go. I left, and the only thing that interested me in our session was the idea of a journal.

*******************************████

Dear Journal,

My stupid therapist told me to get a journal. I had a bunch of them in the hospital. I can tell already that this is boring. So I'll write more later.

    -Mylee Rose

Dear Journal,

I don't want to feel handicapped forever. I should just live in the hospital forever. It's boring as fuck out here. This sucks.

                    -Mylee Rose

Dear Journal,

My counselor is an asswipe.

-Mylee Rose

A week had passed. I was sitting in my therapist's office again.

"So how was your week?" he asked.

"I've been writing in a journal."

"Has it been helping?"

"No."

"Do you have it with you?"

"Yes."

"Do you mind if I read it?"

"Sure, go ahead."

He sat there for a whopping two seconds, because I didn't write much.

"I'm sorry you feel that I am an asswipe," he said.

I almost laughed, but I didn't.

"Have you had your visions lately?"

"It only happens in cars," I lied.

"You can look at this as a writing assignment, I want you to remember the last time you felt really happy, and write about it, and show it to me next week, unless you don't feel comfortable sharing it with me. Have a nice weekend."

****

Dear Journal,

I loved spending time at my neighbor's house. It literally became my new home, and my new family. My friend had two parents that loved each other very much, and a bunch of brothers. I slept over their house as much as I possibly could, to get away the loud fighting in our home.

When my parents fought, it was screaming, slamming things, and breaking things. My sister and I would try not to cry, because if we did, it made my parents scream louder. "Look what you're doing to the kids." We'd have to run away so we wouldn't get blamed.

They fought and blamed us. They tried everything to make it work, but it just wasn't working. My mom never told my father that she loved him. There wasn't even an instance where they spent too much time together, they both worked, and for the literal few hours around each other, they couldn't stand each other. They got married thinking that would solve things.

They had too many unresolvable issues. So, staying over my friend's house shed some light that not every family was like mine. I had fun over there, they had a trampoline, and the house full of boys was funny to me, because I had a sister, and always wanted a brother.

I slept over her house so much that people at school referred to us as sisters. We were so close; we could finish each other's sentences. I never got sick of her. One day her parents were in a Jacuzzi and me, my friend, and all her brothers were swimming in a pool. I forget where we were exactly, but it was peaceful, and the backyard was decorated beautifully. I walked over to her parents while everyone else played like children.

"My parents don't love each other anymore. How do you two love each other so much? Is there a secret?"

The two of them looked at each other and I could tell they felt bad for me to finally let them know the truth as to why I slept over so much. I was exposed and felt vulnerable, but I thought if they could give me the secret, maybe I could fix my family.

"Never go to bed mad at each other," her father said.

I never bothered to give my parents that advice, because I knew they were beyond fixable at this point, so I used it with all my relationships. It was good advice. These two lovebirds were the model of a perfect relationship to me, and I inspired to be like them. I found out later in life they got a divorce.

So I guess my happiest moment, was sleeping anywhere other than at home.

-Mylee Rose

"Mylee this is wonderful, it was very insightful, I feel like I know a little about you, did it help to let out a memory?"

"No," I lied.

"You're an excellent writer, I never would have known! Was this healthy or unhealthy for you?"

"It was corny," I said.

"Your next writing assignment is to find an instance in your life where you think you deserve an apology."

    I must admit, he was going somewhere with this writing stuff, and the assignment idea made it feel like I was back in school, and how much I loved writing. The fact that he wanted to read made me feel like I can let my creative side out. Feeling like somebody actually wanted to listen to me, and care, even if it was for a paycheck, made me super excited to write in my journal.

I left without showing any enthusiasm.

****

Dear Journal,

My therapist wants me to write about why I deserve an apology. Well let me start with my friends. They never really cared about me. We talked on the phone, we hung out, but in the end, I couldn't even trust them for one simple sleepover. Never mind the time when I was just a child, and the girls insisted on having a lesbian orgy. I'm talking about the time when I drank a little too much, and fell asleep, and woke up to being violated, and burned. I hang onto it like a disease, I live life thinking about it every day. I wonder if I would have a great job, a better life, maybe I would be married, maybe I'd be a great mom, a loving wife. Even with an apology I don't think I can ever forgive what happened.

Next let me talk about my parents. They never supported me in the way where a normal parent would say, "Honey it's not your fault." They never asked me to talk about it.

Maybe they didn't want to cause me emotional pain by bringing it up, but instead stuck me in a hospital because they thought it was going to help me get over the pain. They left me there for years. The hospital staff abused me like a horror movie scene, the patients didn't want to hear about my life, they were too self-absorbed in getting help for their suicide attempts, and no one wanted to hear me. No one took me seriously. The doctors hit on me. I was molested in my sleep in my room, the minute I was transferred to the adult unit. My parents left me in there for so long, that I was transferred to an adult unit. My childhood was lost. My sister owes me an apology for making up a disorder that she had severe phobia of hospitals, just so she didn't have to visit me. My ex-boyfriend owes me an apology for hitting me and making me wear makeup. My family owes me an apology for never visiting me. DCF owes me an apology for taking my daughter away without giving me a chance to be a mother.

Last, my ex-girlfriend and ex-boyfriend owes me an apology for leaving me in this world high and dry, taking their lives, without saying goodbye."

-Mylee Rose

"Mylee, you can take my advice any way you want to, take it and leave it, use it, but do me the favor of considering this idea. You will stay stuck right where you are if you believe you will get an apology from any of those people and situations. You might be sitting around, waiting for an apology you will never get. That's a bad place to be stuck, because you'll never grow. I want the best for you, and I think I understand why you are so stuck in the past. Do you feel like getting it out on paper is doing more harm than good?" my therapist said.

"I like writing. I feel like I should burn it after I write it down, though."

"Well you can! Your journal is yours! If you feel like you have to burn it, maybe you are getting out your demons, and burning it is like letting it go?" he said.

"What do you want me to write about next?" I asked.

"I want you to write about why you like to be called Mylee. I figured let's lighten the mood and change it up to something positive."

****

Dear Journal,

My therapist thinks finding out my nickname would lighten the mood. "Something positive." Let me enlighten him. When I was living in that tiny apartment with my mother, I decided I wanted to change my name, because I didn't like who I was becoming. I wanted to perform, so we called it my "stage name." My mother told me to take all of my problems, and write it all out, get it all out and my slang pen name could be "Mylee Rose," slang for "my life." I made poor decisions when I was young to meet people to have sex with online, and I had some dangerous encounters, so I told them my fake name, as a precaution.

    As I became Mylee Rose, it was more of a mask, because I was running scared. As the name change happened, so went my personality. Mylee Rose could be tough, and not afraid. In the meantime the nickname was burying the real me. Every time someone calls my Mylee, it helps me to forget who I used to be.   —Mylee Rose

****

As my therapist read about my nickname, my mind started to drift to another time. My father and mother were arguing in the kitchen about me.

"There's something wrong with her! It's not just the rape, she needs serious mental help," I heard my father on the phone with my mother. They were in the middle of their divorce, but they still talked on the phone.

My family couldn't deal with me. I wasn't like them. Sometimes I wondered if I was adopted.

"Mylee," my therapist interrupted my thoughts, "Do you like being called Michelle?"

"NO!!" I shouted. It was almost as if his words stabbed me.

"What's wrong with Michelle?"

"Please stop saying that," I begged.

"Can you explain who Michelle is to me?"

"Michelle had high honors. Michelle had friends. She didn't care what people thought of her. She was strange, in a good way, she made funny faces, she made people laugh. She was special, she was going places. She had a bright future."

"So what happened to Michelle?" he asked.

"Michelle died," I whispered.

"If you could say one thing to Michelle, what would you say to her, to pull her out of the storm that she is stuck in?" he actually grabbed a chair. "Little scared Michelle is sitting in that chair. What do you want to say to her?"

"I would say don't let anything or anyone hurt you."

"So, why can't you say that to yourself, right now."

"Please stop. I don't want to talk about it anymore," I said as tears swelled up in my eyes. I never cried in front of my therapist yet, and I didn't want to start.

"If you're not ready, I understand. It's a pretty big step to take. Do you know how beautiful you are? I don't mean it in any way except this, I see your scars underneath your tattoos. I see the inner laugh that you carry with you, I see that Michelle still inside of you, dying to come out. I know you are hurting, but when is the time that you can find your inner happiness again? Our next writing assignment is simple. Write ten things you love about yourself. Enjoy your weekend."

I walked out of his office, kicking stones on the way to the bus stop. I was staring at all the people, in a hurry to get where they were going, maybe to their jobs, to their families. I fell asleep so I wouldn't cry again. When I got home, I stared at my journal. I started crying. I looked over at my mirror, which was covered in blankets because I hated to look at myself. For a brief second, I almost made the step to remove the blanket. I couldn't do it.

****

Dear Journal,

He wants me to write ten things I like about myself.

1.

2.

3.

4.

5.

6.

7.

8.

9.

10.

                    -Mylee Rose

It was hopeless. The next day, I got on a bus and rode to my appointment. I watched outside the window where my hallucination haunted me. I took a medication to stop the shaking. I walked to the building, opened the door, and slowly slumped into the waiting area of my therapist's office.

I thought about an old Christmas with my family, and my mother snapping pictures of my sister and me opening up our presents. My father screamed at her "LET THEM JUST OPEN THEIR PRESENTS WITHOUT NEEDING TO TAKE A PICTURE EVERY TWO SECONDS!"

I wanted to scream at him, it was the tradition, my sister and I didn't mind it. Anything they did annoyed the hell out of each other. The Christmas spirit went away, and I didn't want to open presents anymore.

"Mylee, he's ready for you," the secretary said.

"Before we get to the writing assignment, I want to know how you're doing. You look upset, did something happen?" he said.

"I'm fine." I was starting to get used to horrible memories popping up in my head every two seconds. I always thought they would magically go away, but they never did. I tried to stuff them inside.

"So, name the ten things you love about yourself," he suggested.

I handed him the journal, flipped to the page where I wrote nothing. I was ashamed. I told him I didn't feel like talking today and I walked out.

As I headed toward the bus stop to go home, I bumped into someone, and he was incredibly cute. We introduced ourselves, and he told me there was a tent giving out free pizza by the library and asked if I wanted to come with him. We grabbed a slice, I told him it was a cute little date, but I didn't give him my number. I just wanted to go home.

I stared at my journal again when I got home, and this writing assignment for a list of things that I love about myself was too hard for me. I figured if I knew the answers, that I wouldn't need therapy.

I took the blanket off the mirror to make sure I didn't have anything in my teeth and that my hair was okay, in case I bumped into the pizza guy again. I placed the blanket back over the mirror.

I knew I was sinking into a deep depression, but the writing assignments and the chance to run into that guy another time motivated me just a little, to try to smile again. Eventually, I stopped going to therapy. I stopped taking my medication. I turned to alcohol. I gave up on myself, again.

I went through a phase where I wanted to believe I had no mental illness. It went on for weeks. I screamed at both of my parents,

"I was hospitalized for no reason! I could have been normal!"

I was searching again for that apology that I'd never get. After a month or two went by with no meds, I ran out to live on the streets, to find that guy.

When I finally found him again, he became my boyfriend rather quickly, his name was Zach, and told me I was his little Michelle, not Mylee, and he didn't want me to hide anymore. I finally felt like I could be myself, whoever that was.

I began anger management, gambling therapy, and more individual therapy. I never would have pictured me making mature decisions. I knew I needed the help, and I finally began to take my medicine, and to remember to take my medicine.

At first, I couldn't do simple things, like shower, or tie my own shoes. I had other people taking care of me for so long, that my newest boyfriend would do all of the things for me. I met him like a romantic dream, ran into him on the street, and when we locked eyes, I knew this was going to be the one I wanted to spend the rest of my life with.

He helped me get back into therapy, he helped me to remember to take my medicine, he listened to all of my ranting, and he was the ear that I needed all along. I realized that with my diagnoses that depending too much on someone else could become unhealthy. I was so nervous about finally feeling real love, that I asked him to go to couple's counseling with me, as a precaution, and he agreed.

I had chased love like a maniac for so long, looking in all the wrong places, like bars, hospitals, group therapy, meetings. So, when we bumped into each other on the street, I felt like it was a corny romance movie, but I knew I had to hold onto him without scaring him away.

Nothing I said about my past seemed to scare him, even though I had so much baggage. I got lost in the world of drugs again for a while before I met him, so, he helped me quit, and told me how important it was to focus on my children. He was absolutely right. I asked the guardians of my children if I could see them more often, that I was finally sober, hospital free, and medicated.

My babies became my world. I was being so selfish, yes, the word I hate so much. I had a very hard time listening to his life stories, because I was so obsessed with myself, and I started trying to change that. I desperately wanted to be a good listener, and I finally started to feel like "Michelle," again.

In the new therapy groups I signed up for a new doctor that wanted me to go through a series of tests. "I'm going to read you this paragraph and quiz you with 20 questions, so pay attention," said Dr. Ronald.

I had been in this doctor's office for over two hours, and finally the test was over. "Ma'am, you have a very serious case of Adult A.D.D. and A.D.H.D."

I was furious. My entire life I had this problem and my parents never bothered to look into getting me tested for such a fixable problem. Instead they had a bunch of doctors stick as many medicines that they would in my body and make believe I had all these diagnoses to make a fortune off of me. I knew I was a hard person to figure out, but I never believed I should have been in a hospital.

I proved my parents were right, eventually, when

the animal came out of me in Elfwood's walls, but I always wondered if all the extra problems were brought on by the abuse and torment that happened in there. I walked out of the office, and I jumped into Zack's arms and cried.

"Maybe there's not anything really wrong with me baby? What if this whole time I was misdiagnosed? I lost a decade of my life trying to figure it all out. I could have went to my prom, maybe I wouldn't have had to get homeschooled, maybe all my problems were not as big as those doctors made them seem! Maybe they loved my insurance and kept me for a paycheck! I can't breathe right now! I'm so mad!"

"Baby, I love you, and I'm not saying you're parents or that anyone else is right, but when I met you, you were just coming off drugs and you were off medicine for a few months, and I hate to say it, but it wasn't easy for me. These medications changed you, Michelle, and you're somebody new! I promise it might make you a little mad, baby, but you have an illness, whether you want to believe it or not."

His words were kind, and it took a lot of guts to realize he was right. Needing medicine was going to be a part of my life, and I needed to learn how to accept that there was a problem, but that it was fixable, if I would accept and embrace the help.

At the time, I had been in an outpatient day program, with therapy groups for people with mental health and drugs problems, and I loved it, I was learning and benefitting from the program, I couldn't deny that. I didn't want to be mad at Zach, but he was right. No matter what my problem was, the doctors seemed to find the right amount of medication and the correct mixture to help me. I hated the feeling of "needing to be on meds." I wanted to believe I was normal. I had been in denial for years.

I did a lot of thinking, and my mother had paid for a broadcasting school when I got out of the hospital, and I went to the school without being on any medicine, so I couldn't remember anything, none of it. I wanted to go back, as the new me. My school offered the opportunity to go back for free if you were a graduate that was paid in full.

Zach fully supported my decision to go back, and I always felt like he gave me the extra push to commit to the idea. A person can change your life, and you can bump into the love of your life when you least expect it, I am living proof. He even makes me believe and feel like I would have possibly gotten my shit together eventually on my own, without him. He doesn't like taking credit, but I will always feel gratitude for the coincidence that he came into my life at just the right time.

I did waste a lot of my life. I acted like a big baby. My behaviors hurt people, and I didn't care for so long.

Finding love did help, a little, but that's not what saved my life. If you act like an asshole, you're an asshole. I was being an asshole. When I left the hospital and realized it wasn't a big deal, to just go and begin life, that's what made me realize, I wasn't the fucking Queen. I tried to control people, staff, patients, my family, my friends. I was the one that steered them all away.

Being hardheaded, I wanted to blame everyone. I will admit that there were a lot of things that happened that weren't fair. Miss Betty, Mr. Terrible Kisser. There are people, places, things that are beyond our control. I dwelled on it for so long, and cried for too long. The bad stuff maybe made me unlucky, but it didn't make me who I was becoming. I chose to be a monster and act like an animal.

I knew the good, sweet person buried inside me. Love took some of the credit to sweep me back to reality, and sometimes, yes I wonder what would have happened if

I never met him. Would I have continued on the path to self-destruction? Would I have lived in the hospital forever? Maybe I got lucky. Maybe I had angels guiding me out the door. Maybe finding the therapist that knew how to talk to me without pissing me off was the answer?

No matter what, there are no coincidences. I am the person now because it was God's plan. I stepped in a lot of shit on the path to self-discovery. I literally would do it all over again, the same exact way, because that's what it took to find myself again.

****

I was walking down the street to my appointment and I saw a very beat down person that looked familiar, asking people for change. It was the man who hit me in front of a cop and forced me to wear make-up. I wasn't wearing any make-up and he walked over to me, and couldn't recognize me, because he was drunk. I handed him a bus token.

"Thank you, you lovely lady. You're a sweetheart. God Bless." (and I wasn't wearing make-up.)

I'd run into a lot of people after my hospital stays, and they all were completely different people. I never ran into Miss Betty again, because she passed away. I wondered if the reason she was mean was because the hospital turned her that way. I could relate to that, so, I decided to just forgive her. I felt for a long time that the hospital brought out the bad in people. After all, she worked there for so long.

I eventually went back to that kind therapist that thought a journal was going to be a better way to open up a little.

As I sat in my therapists office, I told him that I couldn't write ten things I love about myself, because part of who I am is being insecure, and I couldn't change it overnight, but that I'd work on it. I opened up the journal and showed him my last entry.

****

Dear Journal,

My goal in life was to die. Life seemed like an endless hole that kept getting bigger and bigger, filling up with shit, and nothing was going to make it better. I was so pissed off every time I attempted suicide that I'd have a tube down my nose pumping my stomach, because that means someone saved me, and I'd have to figure out a foolproof plan to die better. I hated being saved. I didn't understand why anyone even bothered. My decision to end my life was nobody's business but my own. If that's what I wanted, let it be, and let me go! Everyone that I hated around me, obviously cared at least a little, to find me, to send an ambulance, but I couldn't see it that way.

I can tell you I don't love me, yet. It may take a while. My boyfriend took down the blankets off my mirrors, and I hadn't looked at myself for years, and I look very different. I feel like I've been through hell, but it doesn't look like it wore me out completely. I can't believe the places I've been, and the people that I've met, or that I can smile. Ten things I love about myself will perhaps take a lifetime to figure out.

I've found gratitude. I am grateful that I am alive. I never thought I could say that, because I've always felt like the world owed me something. My therapist told me that I shouldn't wait for people to come around, that they'll come back around if it was meant to be. I can't beat into my parents head that how wrong I felt they were, and I will never convince my old friends about what happened to me, because I guess they were never friends to begin with if they made me feel like I had to prove my side of the story to them. I don't want to wish bad things on anybody anymore, I really feel like I wasted a lot of time. Now that I'm living in the real world, I appreciate leaves blowing, air flowing, people walking quickly past each other, living their unique lives. I want to do all of the things I missed. I missed my prom, but my boyfriend dances with me. I missed my childhood, but I play with my kids. I missed my daughters' first step, I missed my girls' first haircuts, but I'm here now. I wanted a different future, but I'm gonna take whatever I get. Anything is better than where I was. Ten things I love about myself?

I'm alive. I'm alive. I'm alive. I'm alive. I'm alive. I'm alive. I'm alive. I'm alive. I'm alive. I'm alive.

And I finally appreciate it. We only live once. Is that good enough, Dr. Herald?

-Mylee Rose

****

The best things I could say about my life experiences at Elfwood, is that everything I went through had taught me something. My life may not sound like yours, and maybe you can relate to me somehow, some way. Everyone has something in their lives they would love to forget. We're all people.

I was raped, not because I drank too much. I was raped because not everyone in this world is "all there." You can't trust everyone. I know you don't want to hear that, but it's true. My best friends, who I trusted with my life, my heart, and my soul, took advantage of me in my sleep, and kept going, even after I woke up screaming.

I was hospitalized, because I needed help, I couldn't let go. Without going to groups, and listening to anyone, or the doctors, I couldn't get better. Once help was there, all I needed to do was use it.

I cut myself, because I was lost. I thought I had no

one to help me. I would rather hurt myself, than hurt someone else. I stopped eating because I had no self-love.

In a sick twisted way, I know my parents thought they were doing the right thing by sending me to Elfwood. The decisions I had were to rub their faces in guilt for the rest of their lives, and yes I did my fair share of that, but it wasn't going to solve anything.

I became a monster because I didn't like who I was anymore. People hurt me, teased me, but the only one in charge of my own destiny was me. Sitting in a hospital bed can be a break/vacation for someone, but when it becomes the only safe place left, changes must be made in your life, or it can become your home. Make changes in the people you choose to surround yourself with, changes in your attitude.

It's okay to be depressed, but not to sit in shit forever. Having a diagnosis of psychosis does that mean there is no hope for you. Addictions, depression, anger and mental illnesses can take control of your life, but only if you let it. I let fear take over my life and cripple me for many years. My fear was of the unknown. I wanted to get better, I just didn't know how. I wanted a simple fix, but for me, it took a longer time, because finding self-love is a different length journey for everyone.

Finding love is wonderful, but ultimately, if you can't love yourself, or take care of yourself, finding self-love is more important, because no one can live your life for you. At the end of the day, all you have is you. Are you tired of just surviving? Try living instead. Get unstuck. You have only one life, make it count, starting today, not tomorrow, right now.

There was a very dark time I spent in Elfwood, but I don't like to look at it like there is something wrong with me anymore. I was in a very bad place for a long period of my life, but all it took was opening up and getting help and answers. My boyfriend didn't judge me for it, and my parents still remain in the dark about my complete diagnosis. There are some things I still just didn't want them to know.

My schizophrenia and my child molestation did not have to be a big secret. Holding in problems landed me in hell for a very long time, and something came over me one day to spill the beans. If I feel upset or like I'm about to slip into a depression, I know the right steps to get help. I call my doctor, I reach out to a friend, I tell my boyfriend, I let it out through writing, music, or art, and I know Elfwood is always there, as much as I hated it, it made me who I am today.

I had stopped gambling one day by simply quitting. Sometimes it's just that simple. I'd also been on a medication that increases impulses, and once I changed medicine, quitting was so much easier. I know they say people can switch from one addiction to the other, and my new addiction was "success." Anything healthy that made me happy was my replacement. It took lots of practice, and therapy, to find that happy place.

I hoped one day my children would understand that once I knew they were safe, happy, and loved, that I made the decision to let them stay that way, for their well-being. I thought it was the healthiest thing for them. I always wonder what it would have been like to raise them myself, but I chose the best option for them, and let them remain in their comfortable lives. To me, that was the most selfless decision a mother could make, even if it was difficult.

Unfortunately, the visions never one hundred percent went away for me, but I have a medicine to take that helps control the feelings that come along with the unwanted person in my head. I couldn't really blame anybody anymore, but myself, for the years I lost in hiding.

I could no longer deny that maybe being hospitalized was necessary. Either way it wasn't worth being stuck in that debate forever. I didn't want being confined behind those walls to be my future or my safe place, anymore. So, I left, even though the unknown seemed scary. I guess I chose to "live dangerously" by getting out and choosing freedom.

I came out of hiding, I moved on, and decided to start dreaming, living, succeeding, and smiling, and eventually became the person who I knew was buried in me somewhere. I became Michelle Weir again.

****

The characters and names of the places in this book were changed, as well as the order of events.
Some of it was fictional, but most of it sadly was not. Michelle Weir has not returned to Elfwood, and still attends therapy.

****

For the people in my life who always believed in me, and to my parents, for trying to help me in the best way that they could. Dedicated to suicide, rape, and incest survivors.

You are not alone.

COPYRIGHT ©2016 by Michelle Weir. All rights reserved. No part of this book may be used or reproduced in any manner whatsoever without written permission from the publisher and the author.

Made in the USA
Middletown, DE
22 November 2017